RACHEL

AND

THE NEW WORLD.

A TRIP

TO THE

UNITED STATES AND CUBA.

TRANSLATED FROM THE FRENCH

OF

LÉON BEAUVALLET.

NEW YORK:
DIX, EDWARDS & CO., 321 BROADWAY.
1856.

MILLER & HOLMAN,
Printers & Stereotypers, N. Y.

PREFACE.

A M. H. De Villemessant,

EDITOR-IN-CHIEF OF THE FIGARO.

PARIS, *February* 3, 1856.

MY DEAR M. DE VILLEMESSANT:

I HAVE just arrived from Havana. Here is the latest news: The Rachel company is disbanded. The two worlds are now strewn with the numerous waifs of this terrible shipwreck.

Rachel remains an invalid, on the island of Cuba; not so ill as is reported. Sufficiently so, however, for her to have positively refused to give a single representation to the Antilles. Yesterday a letter was received from her. She will be in Paris in a month and a half, perhaps two months, when the severely cold weather is past.

(At the time we wrote this letter, it was to have been so. Every one knows now that Mademoiselle Rachel preferred to release herself from so prolonged an exile.)

Her sister Sarah left for Charleston. She is going, it is said, to New York, where she wishes to form a company for the representation of comedy and the drama.

Mademoiselles Durey and Briard have also remained in North America.

That country being utterly devoid of amusement, I

preferred embarking immediately from Havana with the rest of the army, on board the *Clyde*, an excellent English steamer, which took us straight to the island of St. Thomas.

We were fortunate, since this island was *enameled* with yellow fever, in being able to take refuge from it, forthwith, on board the *Atrato*, another English steamer, which, notwithstanding terrible weather, and terrific gales that tore our sails and broke one of our masts, landed us safe and sound at Southampton, on the 30th of January, 1856, in twenty days and nights. That was all!

Then how voluptuously we pressed the British soil, with what profound delight we swooned upon a basket of Allied oysters.

Truly, if it were only for the pleasure one feels on landing, it would be worth while to make sea voyages forever. At Southampton, Raphaël Félix, his sisters Lia and Dinah, and M. Félix, their father, parted from us without a tear, and sailed for London. The rest of us embarked precisely where we were; it was much easier, and on the 31st, at four o'clock in the morning, we could have landed at Havre, where, during the visits of the custom-house agent, I caught the most charming cold in the head possible.

Now, my dear Monsieur de Villemessant, do you not perceive, as I do, that the moment has arrived to relate the Odyssey of French tragedy in America? I have come from over there with a volume of anecdotes, of stories, of gossip. A whole volume, you will see! I will confess to you, beside, that it was partly for this that I went there. I had no idea of traversing four thousand leagues in a multitude of countries, each one still more fantastic than the others, to abandon myself exclusively to the tirades of that great Jocrisse, who calls himself Hippolytus, and that false merchant of dates, named Bajazet! Oh! no!

(Here we shall ask permission to insert a little parenthesis—it is the second, and shall be the last—to confess, in all humility, that these by no means literary surnames, granted so cavalierly by us to the two heroes of Racine, have not failed to open under our feet an abyss of most bitter reproaches. Now that we have made this confession, we will risk another—still, in all humility!—that is, that these vituperations have not changed, by one iota, our opinion of the personages in question—they are detestable characters, and we will never give it up. The refractory Hyppolytus is a contraband savage, who no more resembles the son of Theseus than that morose Bajazet is like the Grand Turk! Pardieu! but Racine can well afford to be guilty of those two villainous creations, since he has given us others so beautiful! Besides, to applaud indiscriminately, is to applaud nothing; and to cry up as sublime this "deplorable prince" and his turbaned colleague, is to consider as quite ordinary the admirable characters of Phèdre, Agrippina, Hermione, Clytemnestra—I pass them by, and some even better—to put an end to this *little* parenthesis, which will not finish of itself! We continue the letter to Villemessant.)

I have written about everything, observed everything!

And I beg you to believe that I have a terribly long account to narrate to you since my letter to Roger de Beauvoir—the same that I thank you for having so graciously inserted in your *Figaro*, and which has been translated over there in English, Spanish, and probably in Mohegan and in Red-skin.

Those good Yankees were enraged with me, in the United States. One journal considered it very strange that I allowed myself to say what I did of a country, the only thing of which I did not speak being the language. Incredible assurance, you will admit! As if one were obliged to learn English to have a right to see houses burning, and people disemboweling each other!

To sum up—I am delighted to have visited North America, because it is a duty disposed of, and I shall never have to return there, thank God!

I am delighted to have seen the Antilles and Florida, because they are really splendid and wonderful!

I am delighted, finally, and above all, to have come back to my good city of Paris, for one may well talk and act as if there were only Paris, and there never will be any place but Paris.

So you see that it is scarcely possible to find a man more enchanted than I; yet nevertheless you may put the finishing touch to all those delights, by opening the columns of the *Figaro* to the publication of: *Rachel and the New World.*

I will guarantee that this shall be curious and amusing. This conviction is, perhaps, very pretentious; but, *ma foi!* I have been so far.

I await your reply and press your hand.

Devotedly yours,

LÉON BEAUVALLET.

It will be asked, perhaps, in honor of what Saint have we placed this letter—written two months ago, on our return to France—at the head of this volume.

It is very easily explained.

If we had not addressed the said missive to the very accomplished editor of the *Figaro*—(Bah! let us tell him the bare truth, now that we have no further need of him!)—it is as plain as daylight that Villemessant would not have been able to reply to us: "Your idea suits to a T. Work fast! The arms of *Figaro* are open to receive you."

Without this compliance it would have been quite impossible to have published our tour in the afore-mentioned Journal. Repulsed in that quarter, it is more than likely that we should have been prevented from carrying elsewhere our "gaiters," as well as our accounts of the other world.

The said accounts, not having been published in any journal, our friend Cadot could not have thought for an instant of republishing them, whatever might have been his inclination. And that is why the letter in question, finding itself to be the sole and unique cause of this book, parades so majestically on the first page.

Several days after its appearance in the columns of the *Figaro* (Feb. 14th), H. de Villemessant—already mentioned—published the following note:

"We commence to-day, under the title of *Rachel and the New World*, a great success *de curiosité;* to *Figaro*—who first acquainted the public, in all its details, with the agreement between Mademoiselle Rachel and her brother;—its manager being the first to publish the names and the salaries of the artists who compose the troupe of M. Raphaël; who first made known the sum total of the receipts realized in New York by the Félix family;—to *Figaro* it belongs to relate the Odyssey of which Mademoiselle Rachel has been the Ulysses in America. M. Leon Beauvallet, the Hippolytus of the tragic muse in her chase for millions in the New World, will, at our request, be pleased to give, in seven or eight days, a succinct but complete account of this adventurous peregrination."

It must be understood that it is not this meagre recital that we intend offering you to-day. That would be but a poor attraction, and the leaves of this book would run great risk of remaining uncut.

No! no! this second edition of our jaunt in America has been—we shall not have the presumption to say "revised and corrected;" but certainly greatly increased. Ah! we had already threatened you with these numerous additions; be pleased to remember it, and forgive us for the sake of the intention.

Before closing this preface, observe—I beg, oh! ye

who read prefaces (which, believe me, is a bad habit,)—observe that we have not availed ourselves, for your commendation, of the established address, "dear readers," and that for a very natural reason; because we know nothing falser or more illogical than this expression.

"Dear readers," as if it were not to be read except by intimate friends!

We know, on the contrary, that more than one among you will not fail to heap upon this poor book and its poor author epithets by no means charitable; that is melancholy, but as we cannot help it, we shall resign ourselves.

We proscribe, then, unpityingly, from this volume, the two words in question, and we take this occasion to do the same with those of "beautiful lady readers," an expression as absurd as the other.

If our lady readers are beautiful, they certainly do not need us to tell it them; if they are not, we shall appear, at least, too good to throw in their faces a flattery or an impertinence. Two things equally useless, that we hate as we hate the plague, and from which we fly with all the rapidity of our pen.

That arranged, we commence.

CONTENTS.

FIFTH PART.—RETURN TO NEW YORK.

SIXTH PART.—THE QUAKER CITY.

SEVENTH PART.—SOUTHWARD.

EIGHTH PART.—THE QUEEN OF THE ANTILLES.

NINTH PART.—FROM THERE, HERE.

RACHEL
AND
THE NEW WORLD.

First Part.
BEFORE LEAVING.

CHAPTER I.

WHICH MAY SERVE FOR A SECOND PREFACE IF YOU PLEASE.

It would not have been, perhaps, entirely unsuitable to have begun this little volume by some biography of Mademoiselle Rachel, and by an account, more or less brief, of her previous dramatic tours in France, England, Belgium, Switzerland, Germany, and the Empire of the Czars.

But all that would have made an endless story, and our poor little *diable* of a volume would have become, quite unconsciously, an immense folio!

A dangerous transformation! which would not have failed to have recalled to everybody the famous saying of Perrin Dandin: "Now let us go on to the flood?" That is what we did! And throwing aside the youth of our great *tragédienne*, all adventurous as it was, not giving even a recollection to her numerous excursions in old Europe, we returned naturally and vigorously to *nos moutons* of the *Figaro*, that is to say, to the Odyssey of the tragic muse in young America!

A prodigious, impossible event, about which all the newspapers in the world made it their duty to entertain their readers during three hundred and sixty-five long days—that is, for one whole year! And the last word is not yet said!

Rachel in America!

This news astonished at first; excited afterward!

Such a whim was not to be believed. One could almost pardon all her old escapades, and understand that of St. Petersburg and Moscow; but a voyage to the other world! Ah! for a certainty, that exceeded a joke, and the public began to grumble in good earnest!

If it had merely grumbled; but it was not contented with that!

It was as jealous as a tiger, and wished at any price to avenge itself on this ungrateful Rachel, whom it loved so much and who again betrayed it! And for whom, *grand Dieu!*—For savages!

And see the luck of this Othello-Public! Scarcely had it spoken, ere the vengeance that it demanded with hue and cry, came of itself, in the person of a fair Italian, an unknown, who, by chance, plays tragedy, who, by good fortune, has talent, and who fell from the clouds one fine morning, quite unexpectedly, like the *Deus ex machinâ* of the antique.

CHAPTER II.

WHICH, NATURALLY, TREATS OF RISTORI.

La Ristori! From this moment, to her, to her only, the enthusiastic crowd hurled the bouquets and the acclamations that the imprudent Rachel had dared to disdain! La Ristori!—she became "the great speculation of Paris during the exhibition!" as Auguste Villemot said in one of his charming chats in the *Figaro.*

La Ristori!—"What is she?"—adds the witty chronicler (pardon, my dear Villemot; I rob you like a fellow in the woods). "What is she?"—talent, genius, or an accident? Must her success be accepted according to its intrinsic value, or must we deduct from it the malicious pleasure that seems to be experienced in using it as a battering-ram to demolish the reputation of Mademoiselle Rachel. She, with her disdainful sorties and her triumphal reappearances, finds at last with whom she has to deal. The hostile critic has now a plan of operations, and the work of ruin, begun by sapping, is effected by an infernal train. The synagogue is touched, and the high priest has ordered prayers. I sincerely believe that Mademoiselle Rachel will survive all this; but she will learn from it that one must despise nothing, not even the public—a libertine who dotes on new adventures. "So, either for love of herself, or malice toward her rival," la Ristori found all Paris at her feet. The "rage," a capricious goddess, who, in this country, embraces her favorites even to suffocation, put on her forehead this star of the elect, whose fame has gone forth to the four corners of the globe. "La Ristori! Have you seen la Ristori? Tell us of la Ristori!"

No room for anything else—in prose, in verse, in pamphlet, in conversation, in every formula of human language, a universal consent to celebrate the goddess. M. Jules Janin wrote about her, *inter alias*, a very eloquent article. Only it seems to me that, in the last column of his edifice, he got a little out of breath in showing that la Ristori leaves la

Rachel intact and invulnerable. Our Parisian public always proceeds unfortunately by the means of comparison and exclusion. With the assistance of malignity and reaction, there is no lack of persons who affirm to-day that Mademoiselle Rachel has never recited a hemistich without disgracing it. That recalls a very good repartee of Madame de Stael: A man, who was aware of her spite against the Emperor, said one day in her presence, thinking to flatter her greatly, that Bonaparte had never possessed either talent or courage. "Sir," replied with severity the author of *Corinne*, "you would have a great deal of trouble to convince me that Europe prostrated herself for fifteen years at the feet of a fool and a poltroon."

In our turn, it seems to us difficult to admit that Mademoiselle Rachel should, for fifteen years, have enveloped in a complete mystification the superior intelligences, the press, artists, and the liege public, which knows so well how to defend itself against an attempt to impose on it that which is not to its liking. For fifteen years Maximes and Araldis have been thrown at the feet of Mademoiselle Rachel, to trip her up. She has passed over these manikins in her triumphal march. To-day the case is more serious; la Ristori holds the lyre with seven chords, and of these seven chords of the human soul, Rachel has never touched but two. That is the state of the question. And this gallant *Figaro*, who is just by nature, says beside, in reference to it:

"We are, in truth, overgrown children; after we have amused ourselves for some time with a fine toy, if we are given another, we immediately forget the first; and it is fortunate if we do not break it by striking it against the new one."

We had a beautiful tragic play-thing, Mademoiselle Rachel; the Italians showed us another, la Ristori; *crac!* here we are, at this moment, trying to break Rachel with la Ristori, as if the domains of theatrical art were not vast enough to offer two seats of honor to two women of different but equal talent—the one in tragedy, the other in the drama.

The greatest *brat* of this age, the *papa* Dumas, is one of those who threw away, most spitefully, the Rachel toy for the Ristori toy. It is true that the Rachel toy has never entertained him much in his day. Rachel has played Saint Ybaret too often, and Dumas not often enough; that is his criterion.

The other day, then, Dumas, the papa, witnessed from his box the performance of Marie Stuart, and the enthusiast cried, in his delirium:

"Bravo! bravissimo! that woman is Mars, Lecouvreur, Clairon, Duchenois, Georges, Le Kain, Talma, Kean, Macready—all, united in one single talent! Bravo! bravo!"

Some one near him murmured, timidly, "However, Monsieur Dumas, Mademoiselle Rachel——."

"Eh! Monsieur," replied Dumas, brusquely, "to be able to judge correctly of Ristori's genius one must understand Italian profoundly. Do you know Italian well?"

"Yes, Monsieur Dumas, as you know French!"

"Then," said Dumas, with the most exquisite good-humor, "I said truly, you do not know Italian!"

CHAPTER III.

IN WHICH MADEMOISELLE RACHEL DECIDES TO GO INTO EXILE.

SEEING this rage, this fury, this nameless enthusiasm for the new comer, Mademoiselle Rachel, who, all along, has been undecided as to the proposition of her brother Raphaël, and who had found, each day, some new pretext for not signing, definitely, the American agreement, wished now to leave, as soon as possible, the insolent country which had had the audacity to invent another *grande tragédienne.*

High authority did its best to keep her! It was trouble thrown away. She paid no attention even to her nomination of professor of declamation at the *Conservatoire*, which nomination appeared at full length in the *Moniteur Universel.*

Go, she would!

To effect that, she consented to everything, even to give a series of representations at the

Theatre-Français (a thing which, until then, she had implacably refused).

They say, besides, upon this subject (is it true?—that is the question), that it was not solely to obey the authorities that she deigned to reappear on the French stage, but, partly, to prove to her old courtiers that if they had changed she had not!

And, in fact, she had several truly splendid nights, and, as a quēen still, she left her palace in the *rue Richelieu*.

For a performance of Phèdre, it is said (is it a false rumor?) that she sent a box to her triumphant rival, with a charming letter.

Myrrha hastened to accept both the letter and the box, and did not wait to be begged to applaud.

Ah!" said she, envyingly, "how happy is Rachel! The French understand her!"

Yes, the French do understand her; but she now prefers to them the Americans who, assuredly, never will understand her!

However, if Rachel had not thought of going to the United States, la Ristori would have met, perhaps, in France the fate of Macready and so many others; and if this same Ristori had not been welcomed here as she was, it was also probable that Rachel would never have hazarded her life to go to America in search of imaginary millions, of which she was not in need.

That is so true, that before the appearance of the new tragic star, there was, on the part of Mademoiselle Rachel, perpetual hesitancy.

Every moment, Raphaël Felix, sole director of the transatlantic enterprise, believed that all had gone to the bottom.

The great *tragédienne* had around her many persons who did their best to keep her in her own good France; she, on her part, did not paint this distant pilgrimage in colors so completely rose-hued as to induce her to consent till the very latest moment. At last, wearied of the incessant attacks of the press, vexed with the whole world and herself, a little fascinated (and that explains itself!) by the promises, as splendid as improbable, held out to her by America through her brother, she pronounced the YES, so impatiently awaited.

CHAPTER IV.

IN WHICH MILLIONS ARE SPOKEN OF TOO LIGHTLY.

The day after the signing of the agreement, the following appeared in the *Figaro:*

There is no longer any opposition to the dramatic excursion of Mademoiselle Rachel to America; the day of her departure is fixed, and the bold young Raphaël Félix, director of the *congés* of his sister, has foreseen and arranged everything for the approaching campaign.

Under the title of *petits documents* for the artistic history of our epoch, we publish the authentic engagement which Mademoiselle Rachel has contracted with her brother and director.

Here is, first, a list of the troupe and the budget:

		Francs.
1st.	Mademoiselle Rachel for the whole campaign, - - - - - -	1,200,000
	Four performances, with benefits guaranteed, - - . . - -	80,000

		Francs.
	Hotel expenses, per month, - -	5,000
2nd.	Mademoiselle Sarah Félix, for all the campaign, - - - -	60,000
3rd.	Mademoiselle Lia Félix, do., - -	60,000
4th.	Mademoiselle Dinah Félix, do., - -	50,000
5th.	Mademoiselle Briard, first *confidente*, -	12,000
6th.	Mademoiselle Durrey do., -	12,000
7th.	Madame Latouche, second *confidente*, -	9,000
8th.	Three *femmes-de-chambre*, - -	6,000
9th.	M. Randoux, *jeune premier rôle*, -	30,000
10th.	M. Chéri *aîne*, *premier rôle*, - -	30,000
11th.	M. Latouche, *père noble*, - -	30,000
12th.	M. Leon Beauvallet, *jeune premier*, -	20,000
13th.	M. Dieudonné, *amoureux*, - -	12,000
14th.	M. Chéri jeune, *troisième rôle*, - -	12,000
15th.	Manager, M. Bellevaut. - - -	15,000
16th.	Administrator, M. Gustave Naquet, -	12,000
17th.	Cashier, M. Lemaître, - - -	15,000
18th.	Prompter, M. Pelletier, - - -	6,000
19th.	Three male servants, - - -	
20th.	Hotel expenses for the family, - -	36,000
21st.	Traveling expenses of the company for the year, - - - -	170,000
22nd.	Rent of the different theatres in the United States, and outlays for each performance, - - - -	459,000
23rd.	Unforeseen expenses, - - -	100,000
24th.	Hotel expenses during the month of August, - - - -	10,000
25th.	Indemnity during the closing of the theatres in June, July, and August, 1856, - - - - -	25,000
26th.	Costumes, - - - -	15,000
27th.	Transportation of luggage, - -	8,000
28th.	Installation of *bureaux* in New York. -	7,000

	Francs.
29th. Preparatory travelling expenses of the director, - - - -	42,000
General expenses of the enterprise, -	
Total, - - Fr.	2,554,600

The expenses of this enterprise are, as may be seen, considerable; but the profits will be, we doubt not, immense (we shall see at the end of this volume if the profits have been so remarkable). The motive of our great *tragédienne*, in undertaking this fatiguing voyage, is not so much to increase her own fortune, as to enrich her whole family before leaving the stage. May this good act result in happiness to herself and all her companions! (Alas!)

The Company will take its departure the 11th of August, on board the steamer *Pacific*, from Liverpool.

Before embarking for America, Mademoiselle Rachel will take leave of the English public in London;—she will play there four times, and will realize by her performances 5000 fr.—exclusive of expenses.

CHAPTER V.

WHICH IS NOTHING BUT THE CONTRACT OF MADEMOISELLE RACHEL.

Between the undersigned:

Mademoiselle Rachel Félix, dramatic artist, residing in Paris, No. 4 *rue de Trudon*, on the one part; and Monsieur Félix Raphaël, residing in Paris, No. 3 *Cité Trévise*, on the other;

The following is agreed upon:

1st. Mademoiselle Rachel Félix will give on account of M. Félix Raphaël, *two hundred representations*—tragedy, drama, and comedy—the said representations, as nearly as possible, to be concluded in the space of fifteen months, from the day of the first representation, which is now fixed for the first of next September; in that case, the expiration of the present contract shall take place on the thirtieth of November, eighteen hundred and fifty-six. The representations above mentioned to be given, at the option of M. Félix Raphaël, in the territory of the United States, or North and South America, or at Havana.

2d. Mademoiselle can refuse to remain in "the South" of America if the sanitary condition of the country, into which M. Félix Raphaël would wish to take his company, should be of a nature to affect the health of Mademoiselle Rachel, who reserves to herself the exclusive right of not going to New Orleans, Havana, or Mexico until the fevers shall have disappeared.

3d. Mademoiselle Rachel will have the right to fix the number of representations she will give per month, and that according to the following table.

This table indicates the minimum of the nights that M. Félix has engaged to give to the various directors with whom he has an understanding, as also the maximum of the representations that he has a right to give; in case Mademoiselle Rachel should prefer the maximum, she must each month apprise M. Raphaël Félix of it, in order that he may make the necessary arrangements to insure himself of the houses.

Sept. 1855,	17	repn's, or	21	at the option of	Mlle.	Rachel.
Oct. "	18	"	23	"	"	"
Nov. "	16	"	20	"	"	"
Dec. "	12	"	15	"	"	"
Jan. 1856,	14	"	17	"	"	"
Feb. "	16	"	20	"	"	"
March "	18	"	22	"	"	"
April "	12	"	15	"	"	"
May "	14	"	17	"	"	"
Total:	137	Total:	170			

4th. Mademoiselle Rachel has a vacation of three months, during which M. Félix has agreed to postpone the representations—these months to be June, July, and August, 1856.

5th. Mademoiselle Rachel can obtain the cancelling of the present contract on the 30th day of May, 1856, by forewarning M. Félix Raphaël one month in advance; but it is specified that this rupture shall not be legal unless Mademoiselle Rachel will return to France, with the express condition of playing no more in America, nor in any foreign country, until she has given to M. Félix Raphaël the integral number of representations stipulated in the present contract; she will be permitted to play only in Paris at the Comédié-Française.

5th (*again*). Mademoiselle Rachel can compel the rupture of this contract by paying to M. Raphaël Félix the sum of *three hundred thousand francs, on the score of damages and interest;* besides, she will pay to M. Félix Raphaël the sum of *five thousand francs* for each representation which yet remains to complete the number of *two hundred nights.* On these conditions alone can Mademoiselle Rachel regain her entire liberty.

6th. Mademoiselle Rachel gives to M. Félix Raphael the right of selecting the pieces which shall constitute the repertory for America.

7th. Mademoiselle Rachel will leave Paris during the last week of July or the first days of August, at the option of M. Raphaël Félix.

8th. With respect to the engagements above mentioned, the said M. Raphaël Félix agrees to furnish the said Mademoiselle Rachel Félix with two femmes-de-chambre; to pay the traveling expenses of herself and suite, for the passage from Europe to America, as well as the successive removals which may take place in the United States, in North or South America, or to take them to Havana.

9th. M. Félix Raphaël agrees to defray all

the expenses of Mademoiselle Rachel and suite; these expenses comprising those of hotel, table, and lodging, during the engagement, and the salaries of her femmes-de-chambre at the rate of one hundred and fifty francs per month; a carriage to be placed at the disposal of Mademoiselle Rachel in all the cities where representations are given, the horses and the attendants necessary for this service to be equally at the expense of M. Raphaël Félix.

Mademoiselle Rachel may, if she please, take upon herself all the expenses specified in article 9, receiving from M. Félix Raphaël the sum of five thousand francs per month in exchange for the obligation assumed by the said Félix Raphaël to be responsible for the expenses abovementioned.

10th. Mademoiselle Rachel shall receive six thousand francs for each representation, or twelve hundred thousand francs for the two hundred nights. She will have the right, beside, to four extra representations, which will be for her benefit, the expenses—the rent of the house, the lights, and persons employed—to be reimbursed by her to M. Raphaël Félix;

she shall have the privilege of giving up these four representations to M. Raphaël Félix, who engages also to buy them from her at the price of eighty thousand francs for the four. In case Mademoiselle Rachel should not wish to sell them, she will have the right to choose four cities, to give one of her benefits in each one of them, and at whatever time she pleases; she must give notice a fortnight in advance, each time that she wishes a benefit night. Each benefit will consist of a new play, to be selected by Mademoiselle Rachel.

11th. The said Félix Raphaël binds himself to furnish the said Rachel Félix with all the guaranties and satisfactory bonds necessary to insure to her the payments above-mentioned; after the twentieth representation, Mademoiselle Rachel shall have received the sum of *three hundred thousand francs*, as payment for the first twenty nights; the rest in advance. From the twenty-first representation, Mademoiselle Rachel will deduct from each receipt the sum of six thousand francs, being the amount of her share. These six thousand francs to be each time remitted to her before the commencement of the play, and that to continue until the entire payment of the twelve hundred thousand francs.

12th. Should M. Félix Raphaël neglect to make the above mentioned payments to the said Rachel Félix, she will have the right to refuse to play till M. Raphaël Félix shall be able to pay according to the terms of the present contract.

13th. In case of the indisposition or illness of Mademoiselle Rachel, the latter being sufficient to impede the series of representations she engages to refund, after deducting what would be due her for service performed, the sums she might have received in advance; Mademoiselle Rachel engages, besides, to repay, at the expiration of the present contract, for the time which had been necessary for her recovery; Mademoiselle Rachel to be entitled to the advances returned by her, on the day she shall recommence her performances.

14th. It is stipulated, furthermore, that Mademoiselle Rachel divide equally with M. Raphaël Félix any sum exceeding four millions six hundred and twelve thousand, four hundred francs of receipts, which are to be appropriated as much to the general expenses of the said enterprise as for the benefit of M. Raphaël Félix.

15th. Mademoiselle Rachel affirms that she has acquainted herself with the general expenses, she has shown her approval by placing her signature by the side of the total. It is stipulated, that M. Raphaël Félix shall add a ballet divertissement, the expenses of which are included in the sum, four millions six hundred thousand four hundred francs.

16th. It is agreed between the contracting parties, that the said Rachel Félix shall be free to play, any time she may judge it convenient, for benevolent or Christian objects, either in representations, matinées, or concerts, but that only for the benefit of the poor. It is well understood, that these representations, matinées, or concerts, are to be exclusive of the representations belonging to M. Félix Raphaël, and that Mademoiselle Rachel cannot demand any indemnity. Mademoiselle Rachel binds herself to enter into suitable arrângements with the said M. Raphaël Félix, in order that these said benevolent representations, concerts, or matinées, may not injure the contemplated representations of M. Raphaël Félix, with whom the said Rachel Félix will be always bound to concert, as to the localities and the hours when the said benevolent representations shall take place—for the poor, or the various institutions of the United States. M. Raphaël to have nothing to pay, nor to furnish for them, with the exception of artists from his company —which latter may be demanded of him.

17th. The said Rachel Félix binds herself to play on no one's account, during the engagement concluded by her with the said Raphaël Félix for two hundred performances, with the exception of charitable objects, such as those above-mentioned.

18th. Mademoiselle Rachel will travel, as said in the present contract, at the expense of Félix Raphaël, in the most comfortable manner possible, and she will have a right on all railroads and steam-boats to the first-class accommodations.

Approved, the above document, and the other part.

RAPHAEL FELIX.

The above document approved, and the other part.

RACHEL FFLIX.

CHAPTER VI.

IN WHICH YOU READ OF ANOTHER ENGAGEMENT, NOT EXACTLY MADEMOISELLE RACHEL'S.

SINCE we give you, at full length, the contract of Mademoiselle Rachel, I do not know why we should not also put before your eyes a model contract for a simple stock actor. (N. B.—Compared to Mademoiselle Rachel, everybody is a plain stock actor.)

I have often seen contracts of dramatic artists—I have seen some very strange ones; but, I can certify, that never, never have I found anything so monstrous, as the one you are about to read.

If they were concluding a treaty with a convict going to the bagnio, they could not make the terms more binding

One thing I do declare, and that is, that Raphaël never dreamed of carrying out any one of the articles which he took so much pains to draw up, and have printed in such a magnificent deed.

He knew perfectly well, that, in presence of the law, the whole thing would tumble to pieces, like a card-toy. The company knew it, as well as he did, and that is why they signed the diabolical compact. But it was all the same; one always does wrong in signing such bargains. You shall judge, by-and-by.

The reader is informed that the parenthesis makes no part of the treaty.

THEATRICAL ENGAGEMENT.

Between M. Raphaël Félix, on the one part, residing at Paris, 3 Cité Trévize, and M. ——, dramatic artist—free of every engagement which might interrupt the present one—on the other:

It is agreed, and reciprocally accepted, as follows:

M. —— declares himself *free of every engagement (Bis repetita placent)*, and agrees to play all the rôles which shall be set down to him, of whatever importance, whether tragedy, melodrama, comedy, or vaudeville, in chief or subordinate part, at the pleasure of the management, and according to the following conditions:

He shall employ his talents only in those theatres which shall be designated by the director.

He engages to accompany, in France or abroad, the troupe directed by M. Raphaël Félix; and, to this effect, he cannot claim indemnity for removals, nor shall he have other than the right of transport for himself and his baggage to the place which shall be designated by the management: the weight of his baggage not to exceed one hundred and fifty kilos, any excess to be at his own charge.

He agrees to conform to all the regulations already made, or to be made hereafter ("*To be made hereafter!*" What do you think of that?), and to recognize the authority of persons named by the director, to represent him in his absence.

He puts himself at the disposition of the management from the day of the signing of the present act, whether it be to rehearse or play the pieces in the repertory of Mademoiselle Rachel; or to apply himself immediately to the study of parts which shall be assigned to him. In case of his playing with Mademoiselle Rachel before the date fixed for departure, the actor shall have no right of indemnity; his traveling and hotel expenses only will be defrayed by the management. *Whatever representation may be given before sailing will be considered as* GENERAL REHEARSALS, and consequently indispensable to aid in getting up the repertory, *which ought to be ready before the departure from Paris.* Wherefore the artist must be as punctual in attendance on the rehearsals and representations which may precede the departure of the Company as during the engagement, on penalty of fines to be deducted from his month's salary thereafter. (Not to touch the salary, but to pay the fines—there's coquetry for you!) Absence from three rehearsals, by M. ——'s fault, will justify M. Raphaël in cancelling the present agreement.

The artist agrees not to absent himself nor to lodge out of town without authority from the director; and in this *case* he will indicate the place where he can be found, in *case* he should be wanted; he must be present every day at the theatre at the beginning of the performance (an occupation full of charms !) ready to play off-hand parts in which he shall have appeared already, as often as may be required of him by the management, which by no means implies that the latter will defray the cost of playbooks, nor the franking of passes, which must be done according to rule, under the penalty of a fine of one hundred francs. (Why not a thousand francs ?)

He engages to play every day, and in case of necessity twice a day, (at the same time, perhaps !) whether at Court, (Court in America ! What Court ?) at the theatre, in a matinée, or even in a concert, without the right to claim any compensation (Naturally !).

He engages, moreover, to appear in all accommodation parts which may be required of him, and even as a supernumerary, under penalty of a hundred francs forfeit for each refusal (Well ! that is not dear).

He will be ready to play in all the parts which shall have been assigned to him and in which he shall have appeared before his departure.

The artist must provide all his own costumes

of whatever nature, the management acknowledging no obligation on its part to comply with the usages hitherto in force; the costumes of the artist must be new and always appropriate, according to the part personated by him, they must conform to those of the Théâtre-Français at Paris.

From the signing of the present engagement, the artist shall commit the parts which may be assigned to him at the rate of thirty-five lines a day (thirty-five lines! not one more, not one less!) and shall rehearse as often as the management may judge necessary. He will hand in, conjointly with the signing of the present engagement, the list of parts he already knows in the repertory of Mademoiselle Rachel, indicating also those which he can add between morning and evening.

If M. —— suspends or interrupts his duties for any cause whatever, and especially on account of sickness, the director shall have the right to withhold his salary for each day of such default, with option of final rupture of engagement, should the illness exceed ten days. (Not only have you the discomfort of being ill, but you can no longer touch a sou of your pay. (That is perfect!)

Illness resulting from misconduct, shall cancel the right of engagement. (That is good!) Every artist whom a preliminary certificate does not designate as ill, shall, from the omission of this formality, be considered on hand for that day's duty, and the director may place his name on the bills without special notice.

In case of disputes or difficulties which may be submitted, at the option of the director, either to civil or commercial suit, or to legal arbitration, neither the public representations nor the rehearsals shall suffer by delay of judgment; and, provisionally, M. ——— engages to satisfy the demands of the engagement, or, in default of so doing, to pay for each refusal the indemnity fixed by the regulations.

M. Raphaël knows neither reimbursement nor assignment.

On the arrival of the troupe at the cities wherein Mademoiselle Rachel will perform, the management will be under no other obligation than to transport all the baggage to the theatre. M. ——— will undertake *that* (that what?) of having his trunks removed to his hotel.

The management engages to transport only two trunks, conformable to a model furnished to each artist, (of the eighty trunks in the company, it is well known that there were not two alike!) the latter being under obligation to put his name on each of them by means of a small copper plate.

These conditions being accepted and respected between us, I, Raphaël Félix, engage to pay to M. —— the sum of ——— dollars, valued at five francs, twenty-five centimes, to the dollar.

These payments to be made five days after the expiration of each month.

On the fifteenth of —— next, an advance of —— will be made to the artist which shall be retained by sixths, counting from the first payment, which is fixed for one month and five days after the first performance of Mademoiselle Rachel. The duration of the present engagement will be nine months in America or other states. These months will be: September, October, November, December, 1855; January, February, March, April and May, 1856. During the month of August, 1855, *which is allowed for the voyage*, (counting from the 30th of July, when Mademoiselle Rachel's appearances began in London,) the artist shall not receive appropriations from M. Raphaël Félix for the payment of hotel and lodging expenses. The present engagement to be in force from the embarkation, on the first of August, 1855, (just now the engagement did not commence until the first of September, now it begins on the first of August —a traveling notion!) until the 31st of May, 1856.

Should the management deem it necessary to prolong this engagement, it reserves to itself the right of doing so, and that from a fortnight to a year; in that case, the artist would be notified fifteen days in advance. Should the engagement be extended by the month, the conditions will remain the same as above; if, on the contrary, the extension is by the fortnight, M. Raphaël Félix will pay the artist by the day at the monthly rate.

Should there be a prolongation of the engagement, the artist agrees to remain in America during June, July and August, 1856, without pay, the management reserving to itself the right to suspend operations; during the said three months, M. Raphaël Félix engages to defray the hotel and lodging expenses of the artist at the rate of ten francs a day. It is stipulated that the artist can never leave America, nor even the city in which the company is residing, without written permission.

The immediate rupture of this engagement will be the consequence of any outrage, by word or act, offered to the persons placed at the head of an important enterprise; and this will be at the pleasure of M. Raphaël Félix. (I like that. Why beat, just for nothing at all, a person at the head of an important enterprise?)

As the artist will not be subject to any public début, the management reserves to itself the right, during the rehearsals at Paris, of closing said engagement, should it judge that the talents of the artist are not desirable for this kind of business; the management will also have the right of cancelling said engagement, if between this and the 30th of July next it should find it impossible, on account of circumstances, to conclude all the negotiations with the different theatres with which it is placed in relation; after that time, the artist may consider himself definitively engaged.

In case of war or public calamity, the burning of a theatre or illness—whether of Mademoiselle Rachel or of some other artist—certified by two physicians, all pay is to cease by legal right (that's precise!). Said engagement will also be cancelable if, in consequence of *bad business*, the management should find itself under the absolute necessity of relinquishing the enterprise, and in that case the artist could demand no indemnity; he would be entitled merely to the expenses of the voyage to Paris. If the month has begun, the artist cannot draw his pay, except in proportion for the days that have elapsed. (This is always business-like.) The management would owe nothing from the day on which it should find itself under the necessity of cutting short the representations.

The artist engages to *go to sea* as often as may be required of him by the management, without power to recover any kind of indemnity on that account. (This clause is hard, but logical. For, after all, since one engages to go to America, one cannot oblige the director to take him there in a post-chaise or a wagon—that will come one day, but not yet!)

The present engagement shall be regarded as cancelled, should the representations be interrupted by a command from a higher quarter.

The artist shall give in his name every time that it may please M. Raphael Felix to announce a representation, without which the artist can claim no compensation or indemnity whatsoever.

The present engagement, once signed, cannot be cancelled, save by paying to the management the sum of ———, (the forfeitures range from 25,000 to 80,000 francs—sums equally absurd!) payable by the artist in all lands and under all sorts of jurisdictions, even in foreign countries, so that neither marriage nor *the death of his nearest friends* (that is what one would call providing for everything!), an order for début or enlistment at the *National* theatres of Paris—or, finally, so that, under no pretext whatsoever, can the artist shelter himself to escape payment of the said sum, the management desiring that this contract should have all the force of one drawn up before a notary, in respect of charges, damages, and interest.

Ouf!!!

CHAPTER VII.

WHICH IS ONLY IN CONTINUATION OF THE PRECEDING.

And to say that all you have been reading is nothing to the regulations which complete the thing.

Yes, there are still the "regulations." You might pass them by; but, bah! why so, while you are in the way of them? And, besides, they are well worth the trouble with which they were concocted.

"Hear, people—Hear, everybody!"

REGULATIONS.

Article I.—No artist shall absent himself from the place wherein the company is residing, without informing the management, and indicating the place where he can be found in case of accident or change of spectacle.

Art. II.—The artist who, at the representation, shall keep the play waiting at the precise time for the rising of the curtain, shall pay a fine of ten per cent. on his monthly salary; should this delay continue more than a quarter of an hour, the fine shall be doubled for every quarter of an hour additional.

Art. III.—The artist who shall fail to make his entrée at a performance, shall pay ten per cent. of his monthly salary; if he should miss a whole scene, thirty per cent.; if he should fail of an entire performance, he will be fined the whole receipts, at the highest possible valuation. (In America the largest receipts of Jenny Lind were 93,000 francs. Probably this is the sum which the delinquent would have to fork out. How would he do, that earns but 500 francs a month?—Answer, if you please.) The artist who shall attend the general rehearsal without knowing his part, shall be subject to a fine of five dollars. The fine to be doubled at a performance.

Art. IV.—The artist who, by his own fault, shall retard the representation of a piece announced for a fixed day, shall pay thirty-six per cent. of his monthly salary.

ART. V.—The artist who, by his own fault, shall retard the representation of a piece already played, shall pay one month's salary, the excuse that he had a part to refresh not being admissible. (What memories they must have in America.)

To refuse a rôle, called for in accordance with the provisions of the engagement, will involve a fine of two months' salary, unless, however, the management should think proper to exact heavier damages. (If I were the management, I am sure I should exact fifty thousand livres in stock and a calash with two horses.)

Before an appearance, any artist who is behindhand in that part of his duty shall be *marked* as though he had failed in his rôle. The artist who, on the stage, shall excuse himself from singing in the choruses, shall pay ten dollars fine. (What choruses?)

ART. VI.—No piece which has once been played can be refused in the repertory of the week; and all those performed within three months may be called for between morning and evening, under penalty of a fine of twenty per cent. of the monthly salary of the delinquent artist.

ART. VII.—Cases of indisposition, which shall necessitate a suspension of duty and a change of performance, shall involve an obligation to notify the management immediately, who shall require the illness to be verified, if necessary, and the artist to remain at home, to show himself neither at the theatre nor elsewhere, on the day of such change of programme, on pain of such fine as it may please the management to impose. (That may go a great way.)

ART. VIII.—Every artist who shall suspend duty on account of indisposition, and who, nevertheless, shall absent himself indiscreetly, either at excursion parties or suppers, or to get pupils in town, shall be subject to a retention equal to five times the amount of his salary, for as many days as he shall have *passed* off duty.

ART. IX.—Every indisposition, the feigning of which shall be proved by physicians, shall authorize a rupture of the engagement, and all damages and interest which the management may choose to demand. (That is too fair !)

Art. X.—The rehearsal shall commence precisely at the hour appointed.

The artist who shall fail to answer his cue, shall pay fifty cents (50 *sous*); for a quarter of an hour, one dollar—and so doubling every quarter of an hour until the amount has reached ten dollars.

The artist who shall quit a rehearsal before it is finished shall pay the same fine as if he had been absent entirely. (Then better stay away altogether!)

If the artist is absent at the moment of his cue being called, although he may have already appeared, he shall be subject to a fine of one dollar, and so on, doubling every quarter of an hour, until the amount has reached six dollars.

The actor who shall make it necessary to call him to his cue shall pay, at the third call of the prompter, twenty-five cents (25 sous) fine.

Art. XI.—The general rehearsals shall be conducted with the same care as the representations. At the moment of rehearsing, those persons who shall speak on the stage, or shall remain, having no business there, shall pay fifty cents each time that the stage manager shall request them to be silent or go away. Moreover, no one shall sew, nor do any other sort of work with the needle or otherwise, while rehearsal is going on, under penalty of a fine of five dollars.

Art. XII.—The artist who, missing the hour of rehearsal, shall refuse to come to the theatre when some one is sent to look for him, shall pay a fine of ten dollars, if he has not informed the management since eight o'clock in the morning of indisposition, which compels him to remain at home—the ten dollars not prejudicing the fine for rehearsal. (Oh, no !)

Art. XIII.—The artist who, having at his lodgings a book of the play, shall neglect to send it to the doorkeeper at the theatre, one hour before rehearsal, shall pay a fine of ten dollars. For a public performance the fine shall be doubled. (This article I never could understand—all the artists have play-books at their houses.)

Art. XIV.—The most profound silence must be observed at the theatre after the performance has begun.

The artist who, in the wings, shall speak so loud as to be heard on the stage, shall pay ten dollars fine, and the penalty shall be doubled with each injunction of the stage-manager to preserve silence.

The artist who, while on the stage, whether in the chorus (but what chorus, I say?), or in a simple appearance, shall talk or laugh in a serious scene, shall pay a fine of ten dollars.

Art. XV. — Each artist may have at the theatre one servant, but these servants cannot remain in the wings during the performance; their place is in the top dressing-room of their masters, and they cannot quit it, nor show themselves, without exposing their masters to a fine of one dollar each time that they are to blame. (This may be very dear to the ladies, on account of some slight relations their filles-de-chambre are supposed to have with the foreman.)

Art. XVI.—A table will be placed in the green-room, on which will be announced the work of the day.

Art. XVII.—All discussion foreign to the

business of the theatre is interdicted. Whoever shall violate this article shall be fined twenty dollars.

Art. XVIII.—The costume-department being established only for the benefit of the chorus and figurantes, is not at the disposition of artists, who cannot draw from it a costume for any rôle whatever, the management not recognizing property dresses under any circumstances, even for accommodation rôles. (Be ye, therefore, accommodating!)

Art. XIX.—In any case, when a rehearsal, from whatever reason, does not begin at the hour appointed, the artist must attend; whoever shall quit the theatre shall pay one dollar for a quarter of an hour, and so doubling for such quarter of an hour, until the amount is ten dollars.

The clock of the theatre shall be the only regulator of business. (In all the theatres where we played, either the clock was in a state of complete immobility, or, generally, there was no clock at all.)

Art. XX.—The artist cannot make pretensions to any particular rôle for a début, the management reserving to itself the right to assign these at its own pleasure.

Art. XXI.—Every indisposition which shall last longer than ten days, shall involve a suspension of salary until the artist has returned to his duty. (That's the old story!)

Art. XXII.—It is expressly agreed between the undersigned, that the director has the right to cancel at pleasure the engagement of every artist who shall impede the business of the repertory by bad conduct, or who shall disturb order and tranquillity by quarrelling and mischief-making among his comrades. The same is provided for every case of chronic disease, or improper proceeding; nor can the actor pretend to the least indemnity.

Done in good faith, and signed with full knowledge, after having accepted the terms of the present engagement.

The present act has full force and value, as one executed before a notary.

It is very evident that, as a document, this

engagement deserves, on all accounts, to have a place in this work.

But, I repeat it, Raphaël never meant it seriously; on the contrary, I am happy to be able to say that never (at least in America) did he take from artists a single sou in fines. More than that—one of his ladies having angrily interrupted business for several weeks, she, with his consent, continued to draw her salary without deduction, just as if she had played.

Wherefore, then, somebody asks, all this long string of Blue-Beard articles and clauses?

Mon Dieu! The story will do to laugh at a little. Life is so very dull!

Second Part.

FROM HERE, OVER THERE.

CHAPTER I.

IN WHICH, ON A CERTAIN FRIDAY, THEY LEAVE PARIS.

ON the 27th of July, 1855, although scarcely eight o'clock in the morning, the station of the Northern Railroad was already filled with a curious crowd. Ah! bless me! Rachel does not leave for America every day; and as it is this morning that she starts on this long voyage, they are not sorry to witness a spectacle which they suppose, with good reason, will not be re-enacted very soon again.

All the artists of the company are punctually at the place named by the director.

The families, friends, and acquaintances of the travellers press them to their breasts and overwhelm them with protestations, good wishes, and tears. A scene so touching as to move even the commissioners and gens d'armes.

Raphaël Félix, alone, appeared perfectly happy. With satchel by his side, and cap over one ear, he rushes through the station and the baggage-office, followed by his assistants; having the trunks registered, taking all the tickets, paying right and left, and seemingly as happy as a god! That, however, does not hinder superstitious people from remarking, not without fear, that it is FRIDAY!

Fatal prestige! Ah! ah! a murmur in the crowd: Mademoiselle Rachel gets out of her carriage.

Ah! this time—says the public—she is really going to America! She has often named the time for her departure; but at last she is taking it.

The news of Rachel's arrival is passed from lip to lip; extra couriers run in every direction.

Rachel is going to America! repeats the crowd. There is no longer a doubt about it.

In fact, she has just entered the station.

Two minutes more, and she will be in the car.

But here is something else; at the decisive moment, she changes her mind. She will not leave by this train.

And re-entering her carriage, she disappears from the disappointed crowd, who now sing another tune: Rachel is not going to America. Why the devil did she bring us here this morning?

And each one goes home perfectly convinced that the New World will never hear the declaration of Phèdre or the imprecations of Camille.

Nevertheless, Mademoiselle Rachel does leave Paris the same day, and reaches the capital of England almost as soon as the rest of us.

CHAPTER II.

IN WHICH WE ALIGHT AMONG THE ENGLISH.

It has been well said that London is a superb city; and it is delightful to make one's entry to this giant town by the Thames, which, by the way, is not called *la Tamise*, but the Thames, not altogether the same thing. Besides, it is quite absurd to alter all such names in this way;—when one travels, it should be considered a state affair to recognize them as they are.

It must be understood that we shall not give you the least detailed description of the English capital. That is as well known to-day as the white wolf, and one passes the straits as he would toss off a glass of water.

We shall put aside, then, the custom-house and all that belongs to it; the docks of St. Catherine and the India Company, London bridge and the bridge of Waterloo, which can scarcely be distinguished through the forest of masts; St. Paul's, the Tower, and Westminster Abbey, where rest, side by side, kings, poets, and actors—we shall pass by, without going in, the Colosseum and the Museum of Madame Tussaud, before the Zoological Garden, filled with wonders; go past, on foot, of course, the Haymarket, the Strand, Regent street, and Trafalgar square. In this is erected a statue to the brave Admiral Nelson, in the back of which a lightning-rod is artistically insinuated, which gives it the appearance of having family relations with the statue of the Duke of York, at the entrance of St. James's Park, which statue likewise possesses its little lightning-rod, placed, still better, on the top of his head! The effect is charming!

Bah! do not stop to look, let us walk on—we come to the aristocratic theatre, St. James's, directed for many years by the librarian of Her Britannic Majesty, John Mitchell, an altogether admirable gentlemen, and, moreover, a passionate admirer of Mademoiselle Rachel.

It, therefore, enchants this same Mr. Mitchell

to be able to *respectfully* announce to the English public that *the eminent tragédienne* consents to give four representations at the St. James's theatre, before her departure for America.

CHAPTER III.

IN WHICH THE FELIX ENTERPRISE BEGINS WELL ENOUGH.

On the 30th of July, 1855, an immense placard announces the following performance (we give the programme in English, such as it is. Those who do not understand that lively language, are begged to understand this, all the same):

THE FIRST REPRESENTATION.
(For the first time in this country.)
M. de Premaray's new Comedy of
LES DROITS DE L'HOMME.

Duroc, - - - -	MM. Bellevaut.
Roger de Juliane, - -	" Léon Beauvallet.
Gaston d'Arthez, - - . -	" Dieudonné.
Madame de Lussan, - -	Mlles. Sarah Félix.
Angélique, - - -	" Lia Félix.
Gabrielle, - - -	" Dinah Félix.

After which will be presented Corneille's celebrated tragedy of

LES HORACES.
With the following powerful cast:

Horace, père, - - -	MM. Latouche.
Horace, fils, - - -	" Randoux.

Curiace, - - -	MM. Léon Beauvallet.
Valère, - - - -	" Chéry, jeune.
Flavian, - - -	" Dieudonné.
Sabine, - - - -	Mlles. Durrey.
Julie, - - - -	" Briard.
CAMILLE, - - -	" RACHEL.

PRIVATE BOXES, 3, 4, 5, and 6 guineas (a guinea is worth 26 fr.) : STALLS, 1 guinea : BOXES, 7 shillings (a shilling is worth 25 sous) : PIT (parterre), 5 shillings : AMPHITHEATRE, 3 shillings, 6d.

Rachel is very popular in England, so she produced, that night, a brilliant effect.

The Duke and Duchess d'Aumale, and the Duke and Duchess de Nemours, who were present, applauded with great spirit.

After the performance, the Duke d'Aumale said to Mr. Mitchell, who escorted the prince to his carriage, that "this beautiful language of Corneille, the language of his country, that he had just listened to, had been for him as a fresh rose in a hot spring day."

We have not an exact account of the receipts of this first night; but it is certain that the house was overflowing, and, at those prices, ten thousand francs can be made at the St. James's, perhaps more.

The next day the English press was unanimous in lauding the French tragédienne to the skies, and (what was very kind of it) noticing, favorably, the artists who accompanied her.

The *Morning Post*, among others, was delighted with us all.

Raphaël asked nothing better. This was invaluable as an advertisement in the United States; and all these articles were sent immediately to the other side of the ocean.

CHAPTER IV.

AT THE END OF WHICH MADEMOISELLE RACHEL IS FINED.

On the 1st of August, a second representation at the St. James's:

PHEDRE AND LES DROITS DE L'HOMME.

CAST:

Thésée, - - - -	MM. Chéry, aîné.
Hippolyte, - - -	" Léon Beauvallet.
Theramène, - - -	" Randoux.
Aricie, - - - -	Mlles. Lia Felix.
PHEDRE, - - -	" RACHEL.

Magnificent house, as on the first night.

On the 3d of August, the third representation:

ADRIENNE LECOUVREUR.

CAST:

Maurice, - - - -	MM. Randoux.
Michounet, - - - -	" Chery, aîné.
Le Prince, - - - -	" Latouche.
L'Abbé, - - - -	" Dieudonné.
La Princesse, - - -	Mlles. Sarah Felix.
ADRIENNE, - - -	" RACHEL.

On this night, people were refused admittance. Enormous success.

On the 4th of August, the fourth representation.

ANDROMAQUE.

CAST.

Oreste, - - - - -	MM.	Randoux.
Pyrrhus, - - - -	"	Chéry, aîné.
Andromaque, - - -	Mlles.	Durrey.
HERMIONE, - - -	"	RACHEL.

A smaller house, and much less enthusiasm than yesterday. However, we certainly ought not to complain, and we do not complain ; the proof of which is, that instead of giving only four representations, as was announced, we shall give on the next day, that is to say, the 6th of August, a fifth performance, to consist of

LADY TARTUFFE.

CAST.

Le Maréchal, - - -	MM.	Chery, aîné.
Hector de Renneville, - -	"	Leon Beauvallet.
Destourbières, - - -	"	Latouche.
Leonard, - - -	"	Randoux.
Madame de Clairmont, - -	Mlles.	Sarah.
Jeanne, - - - - -	"	Dinah.
MADAME DE BLOSSAC, -	"	RACHEL.

This play of Madame Emile de Girardin pleases the English public wonderfully.

This character is, however, one of those which, in her whole repertory, Mademoiselle Rachel most abominates. *Madame de Blossac* is completely odious, and this rôle, in spite of Mademoiselle Rachel, produces plainly much less effect than the others. Nevertheless, everybody was called out after the fifth act, and even after the fourth, in which Rachel doesn't appear. Notwithstanding her dislike of this play, this was not the first time that Mademoiselle Rachel had played it in London. Three years ago the piece was performed several times. I remember a good joke on this subject. In the playbills the following appeared in large letters :

"This evening will be presented the new comedy of Madame *E. de Girardin*, LADY TARTUFFE, by *MM. Scribe et Legouve.*"

Two days after the night of the 6th of August, the performances at the St. James's Theatre were closed, by a second representation of:

ADRIENNE LECOUVREUR.

which drew as full a house as at first.

Unfortunately, this piece, which had gone off so well the other night, was, this time, performed in a disgraceful style.

The accessories were forgotten ; no one could recall his proper replies; Mademoiselle Rachel, yes, Mademoiselle Rachel herself, memory incarnate, knew not a word of her part. She separated, she clipped short, she hacked in pieces that poor prose which couldn't help itself:—moreover, in the third act she kept the audience waiting nearly five minutes for her entrance.—And in the theatre five minutes is terribly long.

At once Raphaël mounts his high horse, and, seizing by the fore-lock this occasion to prove to the world that his directorial power was not merely a word, he fined the great tragédienne! Yes, fined her, like the most common martyr! And that is not all, he had this terrible arrest inscribed on the fire-place panel in order that even the lowest boy in the theatre might read it and tell it to his friends and acquaintances. (We must hasten to say that this fine, which was of 100 francs, *pardieu!* was not paid any more than others. At least, if it was, we never heard of it.) To end this deplorable night properly, Randoux, who played Maurice de Saxe, stumbled, on entering at the fifth act, over an iron curtain-rod and was thrown at full length on the stage, disappearing in the prompter's hole.

CHAPTER V.

IN WHICH WE PLAY IN LONDON FOR THE LAST TIME.

On the 9th of August, Mademoiselle Rachel consented to play at the Theatre Royal of Drury Lane, for the benefit of the French Society of Benevolence.

This institution is placed under the patronage of the Empress Eugénie, and presided over by the French ambassador. The representation, patronized by the Queen of England, was distributed after the following programme:

LE DEPIT AMOUREUX.
By the Artists of the French Company.
LE SONGE D'ATHALIE,
By Rachel.
Grand Vocal and Instrumental Concert:
Duet of the *Pre aux Clercs,*
Le Cantique de Noël.
Fanfare Militaire.
Aria: *Love Rules the Palace.*
Le Muletier de Calabre.
Cantate: *La Guerre.*

Sung by M. Blondelet, du Théâtre Royal, Adelphi (with

the permission of Mr. Webster), in the costume of a French Zouave.

During the entr'actes,

GOD SAVE THE QUEEN,
and
PARTANT POUR LA SYRIE.

To end with the 2nd act of Wallace's Opera:

LA MARITANA.

(The poetry of which is simply the English translation of *Don Cæsar de Bazan.*)

Prices of Seats: Stalls, 10s. 6d.; Circle, 5s.; Second tier, 2s. 6d.; Parterre, 1s.; Gallery, 1s. Private Boxes, four guineas.

This performance was very fine, and very profitable, the receipts amounted to 18,000 francs.

That which produced the greatest effect during the evening, was, not the tragedy, nor the concert, nor the comic opera; but the *God save the Queen*, and, after that, the air of Queen Hortense.

Frantic applause, never-ending bravos, and, from the first to the last notes of these two pieces, the audience remained standing and uncovered. A token of the profound respect which the English cherish for their Queen, and of sympathy for their allies.

After this representation, the last which Rachel gave in this city, a charming woman, half English, half French, who resides in London almost as much as in Paris, and who makes it her duty not to miss seeing a single one of our tragedies (which proves her strength of character!), Madame Doche, finally (why could we not have had the naming of her?) came to bid adieu to the great tragédienne, and to wish us all a safe and pleasant voyage. We begged her earnestly to accompany us; but she obstinately refused; she was very wrong! Her sister, Mademoiselle Plunkett, refused also to go to America. Raphaël, however, made her very liberal proposals.

For you may have noticed, in reading the contract of Mademoiselle Rachel, that Raphaël would not have disliked to bring, along with his tragic troupe, a whole corps de ballet. He deceived himself a little, as will be seen, about this grand American public.

Unfortunately for him, this project, which was good, could not be realized, not only on account of the refusal of Mademoiselle Plunkett, but because a *superior will* opposed itself (so they said) to the installation of Terpsichore in the domains of Melpomene. (A little mythology is of great use!)

Before quitting London and its theatres, we cannot refrain from saying a few words about the much-to-be-regretted event which has robbed London of one of her finest theatrical houses: Covent Garden no longer exists. It has been literally devoured by the flames. The fire burst forth during a masked ball, bringing to a close a kind of carnival performance, given by a certain Professor Anderson.

The most unhappy fact connected with the occurrence, is, that the dramatic library of this theatre was entirely consumed.

The loss of the original manuscript of the *School for Scandal*, by Sheridan, is most deeply regretted.

Moreover, it is astonishing how easily the London theatres are destroyed by fire. In 1762 and 1809, Drury Lane was burned; Her Majesty's, in 1789; the Panthéon, in 1792; Astley's, in 1794, 1803, and 1841; Surrey, in 1805; Covent Garden, in 1808 and 1856; Royalty, in 1826; English Opera House, in 1830;

Olympic, in 1849; in 1850, it became the turn of the Argyle Rooms; and that of the Pavilion, in 1856.

How many millions gone in smoke!

CHAPTER VI.

IN WHICH WE MAKE THE ACQUAINTANCE OF THE "PACIFIC."

You will be little surprised, when we say that, at the moment of leaving London, all the irresolution of Mademoiselle Rachel recommenced in the finest fashion, and that the American campaign was once more on the point of stopping short.

Finally, after frequent parleys, we took the railroad for Liverpool, on the morning of the 10th of August, and, that evening, we arrived at that quite important city, in the county of Lancaster, which does not prevent it from being slightly dirty, and terribly smoky. True, it possesses a magnificent harbor, constructed at the mouth of the Mersey, which is some compensation. There, for the first time, we had the signal honor of being face to face with the famous American steamer, which would take us to the other world.

The other world! There is something sinister in those two words!

Happily this magnificent steamer is called *The Pacific.*

That blessed name gives us a little confidence.

Notwithstanding that, however, we generally sleep badly all night.

We dream, pleasantly enough, of Robinson Crusoe, of his desert island, and of his man Friday. At six o'clock in the morning, we get up.

The rain falls in torrents. The aspect of the city is the saddest in the world, notwithstanding the bright yellow bills which decorate the walls, announcing to the Liverpool population (which doesn't look as if it were greatly excited thereat) that to-day Mademoiselle Rachel will take flight towards the other continent!

At nine o'clock we are in the harbor.

The rain continues to pour, with even ludicrous persistency. Decidedly, it rains too much in England! A little steamer takes us to the *Pacific*, with other passengers.

Several ladies are already sea-sick. Fine prospect!

Mademoiselle Rachel says not a word. She is very pale, and seems to be suffering.

We near the *Pacific*, whose black and red chimney already smokes vigorously.

All the travelling equipage is on deck.

A kind of staircase is let down, which fits on the deck of the little steamer.

The general procession moves off. The passengers, one by one, climb the steps with despairing slowness.

It would be a wonder if any one could look cheerful; Raphaël is the only one who is always radiant!

And there is good reason for it; in spite of the Comédie-Française, in spite of critics, in spite of all France, in spite of Mademoiselle Rachel herself, it has come to pass, there is no further question about it! While his sister pale and silent, ascends the long ladder which takes her to the deck of the steamer, Raphaël's joy increases perceptibly.

Finally Rachel is on board!

This time, no one will gainsay it! An agent of Mr. Mitchell, who has accompanied us thus far, seems much moved. He murmurs *vive Ra-*

chel! very low, as if he were afraid of being heard. The fact is, scarcely any one does hear him.

The small steamer leaves us. The farewell scene begins, waving of handkerchiefs, smiles, tears.

We are off!

We begin seriously to believe that Rachel is going to America.

At ten o'clock in the morning the *Pacific* fires off guns, the infernal machine below begins to howl, the immense wheels turn on their axis, and our ship sails for the new world!

CHAPTER VII.

HOW THEY EAT ON BOARD.

THE weather is now superb.

The sea is calm. Our steamer flies with frightful rapidity, notwithstanding the enormous freight with which she is loaded. She is one of the best vessels of the company. So much the better! At the sight of this magnificent ship, which glides over the sea, or rather the tranquil stream, wrinkles are smoothed out of one's forehead, and we think only of resigning ourselves cheerfully to our lot. We chat, we laugh, we sing.

Every one now is even foolishly gay. There is only one passenger who does not seem to enter largely into the general cheerfulness.

The poor fellow is dying—at least so it appears, for he is frightfully pale and emaciated.

While we are on deck, a kind of idiot comes out of a little glass cage, behind, and with a sort of hammer, strikes eight vigorous blows on a bell near him.

They inform me that this man is in the enjoyment of his senses, which surprises me, and that he comes merely to indicate that it is noon on board.

Eight blows on a bell for noon! That is ingenious, you will admit.

Scarcely has the last blow sounded, when we hear below an unparalleled uproar.

We think that the boiler is bursting.

Not the least in the world!

It is nothing but the gong.

With this fantastic instrument they indicate the hours of the meals on board American steamers.

We go down to the dining-room, to lunch.

This room, though very large, is literally jammed. Every one disputes his place. All the passengers, without exception, have responded to the call.

They devour.

The waiters look on this scene with a malicious smile, which seems to say, Go on, my little children, eat! Give yourselves up to gayety to-day! to-morrow we shall hear another story from you.

The smile of these waiters frightens me, and I foresee all the horrors of my future position.

At four o'clock, the idiot again strikes eight blows.

The gong sounds again!

It is for dinner.

I confess that I have waited for this moment with a certain impatience.

At lunch, not knowing a word of English, I had not been able to get myself waited upon, except by the means of pantomime, more or less expressive, and I must say that I was dying with hunger. To say nothing of the fact that many travellers had greatly applauded to me the cookery on board American steamers, *ma foi!* I was marvellously well prepared.

Alas!

But let us not anticipate events!

At first, all the service is conducted by the sound of the gong, which is by no means amusing.

They entertain for this Chinese instrument an inexplicable tenderness. Why? I can't say.

I suppose it aids their digestion.

First blow: Soup is served.

This soup being ornamented with coarse pepper and bits of meat, I denied myself.

Second blow: All the silver covers on the dishes are removed.

If you but knew with what rare precision, with what perfect unanimity, these waiters uncover, at last, the numerous edibles so carefully hidden!

Once or twice I tried, before the blow on the gong, to see what was under the cover next me; but the waiter leapt to my side as if to devour me.

Naturally, I believed this food of which they were so careful was exquisite.

Ah! well, yes!

Vegetables cooked in water, after the English fashion; meats killed in advance and preserved in ice, consequently without taste or savor.

Beef, mutton, fowl, all having the same taste.

Atrocious!

It is well understood the wine is an extra. For a great deal of money you have a right to expect a very little wine.

Generally the Americans drink only iced water during the repast. They make it up well at dessert with numerous bottles of Champagne.

I have noticed that they are very fond of champagne. They have a right to be ; a still better reason is, that nearly all of them are members of a temperance society.

CHAPTER VIII.

IN WHICH IT IS SHOWN THAT THE DESSERT IS STILL MORE DISMAL THAN THE DINNER.

One might suppose that to announce the entremets, they would dispense with this *diable* of a gong.

Not so. It sounds then, more than ever.

Then defiles a long string of nameless cakes, impossible puddings, and extravagant pastries.

They mix rice with rhubarb, cream with gooseberries *à maquereau*, currants with long peppers.

It is a culinary hodge-podge inconceivable. One's palate is completely perplexed by these strange and unnatural marriages, so much so that, though we taste all, we can swallow none.

(N. B. I do not speak here of the Americans; they find everything very good and eat of all.)

I decide to take a piece of a cake a little more civilized than the others, but at the moment I am about to take it, the eternal gong sounds again and all the cakes disappear as if by magic.

Not contented with taking off the dishes, they carry away the cloth.

I think that dinner is over; I rise.

Not at all.

A procession of waiters sallies forth from the pantry with baskets of oranges, plates filled with walnuts, hazelnuts, almonds, and other fruits equally dry.

I sit down again.

Two waiters place themselves at the end of the table.

As they continue to hold the dessert in their arms, I extend my hand and try to take an orange.

The same pleasantry recommences.

The waiter recoils, frightened as the flood from Theramène, and he makes a frightful grimace at me, which would cause him to be mistaken for the illustrious guardsman called Jocko.

Last blow of the gong.

All the dessert dishes fall at once on the tables.

It is a comic achievement.

Champagne flows, brandy and coffee circulate in every direction.

All are as merry as larks.

The conversation becomes animated.

English, Germans, Spanish, Italians, Chinese, French, Iroquois, Algonquins, all talk together and at the same time. No one understands a word of what his neighbor is saying to him.

It is a terrific charivari, a confusion of tongues utterly indescribable.

I am quite flurried, and, as I have drank a little champagne, I close my eyes, and for five minutes I positively believe myself to be in the tower of Babel.

I await the thunderbolt which will put an end to all this.

I did not wait long.

The bolt burst in a side room; the invalid of whom I spoke above, received it upon his head.

The poor fellow gave up his last sigh at the moment the last bottle of champagne was finished. It were scarcely possible to finish more sadly our first day on board.

CHAPTER IX.

IN WHICH THE "PACIFIC" COMMENCES HER FROLICS.

VERY early the next morning, indeed I may say a great deal too early, the sailors took malicious pleasure in waking us by washing the deck.

Ah! how boisterous they are when they wash the deck, to say nothing of their furious passion for singing, which, joined to the noise, makes them intolerable to the passengers who wish to sleep.

We were now in St. George's Channel.

These quarters being rather rough, the *Pacific* commences some very giddy evolutions.

That affords us comfortable anticipations.

Heads are no longer on their ordinary axis.

The dining saloon becomes empty at a rapid rate. Those scamps of waiters, how well they knew that!

We very willingly remain in the open air, in the after part of the ship.

Until noon, we coast along the shores of Ireland.

These shores, notwithstanding their perfectly wild and desolate aspect, are very far from wanting a certain picturesqueness.

And yet I do not know if it is because these arid cliffs, against which the waves of the sea dash furiously, are the last land that can be seen from here for a long time, but you feel, in a manner, fascinated by them, and, in spite of yourself, you still look for them, even after they have totally disappeared from the horizon.

Mademoiselle Rachel is not very cheerful. In proportion as we go forward her sadness seems to increase.

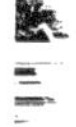

From this day, she remains almost entirely shut up in her state-room.

She is royally ennuyée.

She is never very sick at sea, but almost always ill at ease, which is worse.

What an odious thing a voyage is! The sea is decidedly one of the most frightful torments that I know of.

And yet we are on one of the finest steamers in the world. What should we say if we were travelling in a ship?

The engine, or rather the engines—for there are two, in case of accident—on these immense steamers are truly admirable.

Nothing can be more interesting than to examine them in all their details. It is enough to set one crazy.

In the engine-room one might imagine himself in the bottomless pit; and still more readily believe it, because the firemen will answer perfectly for your gang of devils.

What queer specimens one sees among them; what wild countenances!

They are all half-naked, blackened by the smoke, as hairy and tawny as beasts; they have long, neglected beards, which conceal their faces, and hang down to the middle of their breasts.

And all of them go and come, run up and down, throw themselves violently among millions of flying wheels, running gear and iron rods, which work incessantly, and seem ready every second to pulverize them.

Seeing them thus going from one furnace to the other, their bodies stooping over the flames, which illuminate them with a strange, fantastic light, it is impossible, I repeat, not to take them for a gang of devils busying themselves in roasting a cargo of the damned.

Add to this the fact, that in this place the heat is awful; that it suffocates, stifles you, and would end by melting you, if you should remain.

How these men can live there is a wonder to me.

Another incredible thing is, to see this immense mass of iron and steel, this giant machinery of enormous weight, dancing as lightly on the waves as a cork or a bit of straw.

That is, besides, the worst of the affair; for when the machine which occupies the centre of the ship amuses itself with such gymnastics, the ship also is forced to execute a terribly shaky polka.

One day, a desperate pitching.

The next, a frightful rolling.

The day after that, for a variety, both together—rolling and pitching.

This is delightful! and so much so, that all the passengers are dreadfully sick!

What the devil are they going to do in such a scow as this?

CHAPTER X.

IN WHICH WE CHAT OF THE BOX AND THE FLAGEOLET.

After we have been several days out, Captain Nye (a perfect gentleman, and an excellent sailor) presents to Mademoiselle, on the part of a citizen of New York, a superb mahogany box.

The sender desires to be anonymous.—What is the mystery?

Let us hope that the future will clear it up.

But what is in the box?

Jewels?

Go to! jewels? they are too common. Better than jewels. Some American perfumery, that is all!

And no means of finding out from whom emanate all these sweet smells! how provoking!

In spite of the present of the unknown perfumer, Mademoiselle Rachel still refuses all recreation on board this good *Pacific.*

She continues to keep her state-room.

Many passengers do as she does, and your servant imitates them.

Raphaël Félix is one of those rare travellers who resist the allurements of the Atlantic.

He doesn't care for the Atlantic. All he thinks about are the dollars of the United States and the pesos of Havana.

As for myself, dismally stretched out in the badly stuffed drawer which serves me for a bed, I think nothing of this wealth in the perspective. I have other things to do.

While I toss in my ridiculous bunk, there steals from the state-room in front of mine a kind of French air on some sort of a flageolet.

A passenger, a friend of the fine arts, perches there.

When I am very sick he plays a very lively air; when I get better, he commences a melancholy, gloomy one.

This flageolet, besides, is quite original. In the midst of his air I hear him occasionally stop and . . . .

. . . .
. . after which, he takes up the air just at the note where he left off.

A good many waiters, generally very hurried and very accommodating, are at the disposal of passengers who are too ill to leave their state-rooms. They bring them their food in a sort of China porringer. Onion soup and fried potatoes are very popular.

Doubled up in this way in these uncomfortable boxes, the passengers have exactly the appearance of great dogs who have the distemper, and whose porridge is brought to their kennels.

Sorry resemblance !

CHAPTER XI.

TOO FOGGY.

On the 18th, at six o'clock in the morning, we are off the coast of Newfoundland.

The great Sand-bank off which we are now passing is famous for the incalculable number of codfish that collect here.

In spite of the frequenting of these peaceable fish, these quarters are very dangerous.

It is here the horrible shipwreck of the *Arctic* took place.

The recollection of this serves only to give rise to thoughts still sadder than before.

Thick fogs surround the ship on every side.

One can scarcely distinguish the top of the masts.

Every preparation is made in case of shipwreck.

The life boats are uncovered and provided with ropes and oars.

The alarm-gun is ready to fire.

The alarm-bell is on the bridge.

All the time that we push on through the fog the captain keeps watch.

The steamer's speed is relaxed; she seems ashamed of her new pace.

All the passengers take advantage of this to come out of their state-rooms.

They are, for the most part, not a little alarmed.

One of them blows up his life-preserver and fastens it around his waist.

He sleeps with it so all night, and it frets him, so that he cannot close his eyes. One thing about it is consoling, that it would have been worth nothing at all, even if we had been wrecked.

During the day, we double Cape Race, which is the most dangerous point. The passengers begin to breathe again. Unfortunately, a melancholy event saddens our evening.

A young calf, brought from Liverpool by the captain, dies, from the effects of prolonged sea-sickness.

His remains are thrown into the sea: a famished shark dines off him.

Poor little calf!

The next morning, when we awake, we have left the banks of Newfoundland; the fogs have disappeared; a dazzling sun lights up the waves, the masts, and the rigging.

The deck is filled with a crowd of passengers, whose presence on board had not been even suspected.

For ten days, these unfortunates have been inlaid in the sides of this frolicksome vessel. Haven't they a right to enjoy themselves?

We perceive, not far from the ship, two enormous whales, who are gambolling on the bosom of the briny waves.

Millions of all kinds of fish appear on the surface, and seem delighted to see us pass.

The appearance of the water changes now, from one quarter of an hour to another.

The ocean is unusually calm.

That may be perceived, above all, in the dining-room, which begins to be filled, exactly as on the first day—even fuller than then.

We find ourselves face to face with furious appetites.

The horrid edibles, heaped up on the table, disappear with fearful rapidity.

Are they famishing?

In the evening, after dinner, an old Protestant clergyman holds service in the saloon.

A splendid sunset puts a glorious end to this day, and makes us forget, in one moment, all the misery to which we have been subjected for the past eight days.

In less than an hour, the sky changes its color and whole appearance more than a dozen times. All imaginable tints, from that of melted gold to the deepest blue. Truly splendid!

A curious effect, and one which I remark particularly, is produced this evening—a perfect circle formed by the horizon, of which our ship is the central point. We have made good progress, yet we are always in the middle.

We seem to sail in a huge basin, over which is placed a great blue cover.

This comparison is, perhaps, not very poetical; but it is a good one.

In the evening, a steamer passes close by

us. Some little sailing craft are distinguished in the distance, and are vividly painted against the fiery sky.

Life comes by degrees.

The temperature undergoes a complete change.

Yesterday, off the banks of Newfoundland, we were shivering: to-day, we are too warm.

The sea-gulls begin to fly around the ship.

We smell the land.

CHAPTER XII.

THE LAST DINNER ON BOARD.

THE 20th is as lovely a day as its predecessor. The sun is more and more brilliant; the sailing vessels still more numerous.

Schools of porpoises romp at a little distance off.

These cetacea seem to be of an exceedingly gay character.

For the first time in ten days, the ship stops. A signal is set for a coast pilot.

He comes alongside, and the sailors hoist him on deck with ropes, like a mere bale of goods.

His arrival exhilarates the whole ship. It proves that to-morrow we shall be at New York.

I need hardly say that the engine, furious at being stopped, even for an instant, starts off again, almost before the pilot has touched the deck.

We go ahead under full power.

It is plain that the horse smells the stable.

The earthy odors grow plainer. American atmosphere begins to prevail. The heat is dreadful, and offers magnificent coups-de-soleil.

Every woman has her own.

A little further on, we see two water-spouts spurted above the waves. There are two whales.

What are they talking about?

But, hush!

The idiot strikes eight on the bell. That is to tell you that it is four o'clock.

Four o'clock! it is the hour of torment—of dinner, I should say!

The last that we shall take on board. Heaven be praised!

It is what they call the Captain's dinner.

This time everybody attends.

Mademoiselle Rachel herself decides to leave her state-room and take her seat at the table beside Captain Nye.

Apart from the champagne, added gratis to the usual bill of fare, this dinner doesn't differ much from the others, which is a misfortune for those who like something fit to eat.

In fact it is the last dinner!

A toast to Captain Nye is proposed. It is drunk with all the honors.

A fair young man, after that, proposes the health of the ladies. His toast is not so successful as the other.

That surprises me. I had been told that Americans were models of gallantry.

Finally, Mr. Stewart (a dry goods merchant of New York, worth forty millions, in the usual style of that place,) toasts the arrival of Mademoiselle Rachel in New York.

All eyes are turned towards her. A *speech* is expected.

But, as she does not understand English, save very imperfectly, she does not reply, but merely bows.

If not she, then her brother will respond. And the general gaze is turned upon Raphaël Félix, director of the *French Company*.

But Raphaël doesn't respond any more than his sister; so neither of them responds, which seems to disappoint the Americans exceedingly.

Not to respond to a speech, is an unpardonable thing among them.

CHAPTER XIII.

IN WHICH THE MARSEILLAISE APPEARS ON THE TAPIS.

Appointing himself master of ceremonies, a French passenger arises and, in the name of the Americans, who never dreamed of such a thing, asks his countrymen to strike up in chorus *la Marseillaise*.

These, not knowing by heart the national hymn of France, turn up their noses at this unexpected demand, and unanimously refuse the honor.

But, here is the best of it.

The passenger turns to the guests and says to them (in English, *ma foi!*) that the French Company declares itself ready to accede to the general request.

Here is an ambush. How can we get out of it? Who will sacrifice himself?

Every one now has his eyes fixed on these

unhappy Frenchmen, who would give anything to be elsewhere.

Time goes on—nobody begins.

Low murmurs are mingled with stifled laughs.

Decidedly the French will not be in odor of sanctity among these gentlemen of the other world.

Finally, oh! happiness! a savior presents himself.

A creole from New Orleans—an excellent fellow, who knows us all.

He knows the *Marseillaise.* He will sing the couplets; the Frenchmen will have only to take up the refrain in chorus.

So he sings the first couplet. He is much moved—which is a bad thing in singing the *Marseillaise.*

Happily the Frenchmen strike up the refrain and give smiling faces to all the guests.

I have heard a great deal of singing in my life; I have been present at many grotesque concerts; but never, never has more uncouth music stunned my ears.

I could have rolled on the floor with laughing—not one singer in harmony with another.

It was so curious, that each one seemed to be singing a different air.

It is scarcely necessary to say that they passed at once to the last couplet—

"*Amour sacré de la patrie!*"

Poor Country!

This last couplet had exactly the same fate as the first.

As to the refrain, it was, if possible, more ludicrous, more extravagant than the other.

So that this little musical fête, which threatened to take a slightly political turn, finished by loud peals of laughter, which, going up the hatchways, awoke even the cabin-boy asleep in the top.

CHAPTER XIV.

LAND! LAND!

MADEMOISELLE RACHEL presented the Captain with nearly two thousand francs, to be distributed among the crew of the *Pacific*.

She gave eight hundred francs to the orphan children of the sailors.

An American lady, seeing her in a generous vein, came to beg her to give them a few scenes in tragedy.

Mademoiselle Rachel refused decidedly.

As she came to America precisely in order to give scenes in tragedy, the lady in question will have an opportunity of hearing her quite at her ease—by paying for it, be it understood.

Raphaël Félix is in such impatience for the arrival of this happy moment, that he signalizes land before any one else.

Unfortunately, what he takes for a lighthouse, is nothing but the lantern of a steamer bound to New York.

Not until midnight do we see land. Everybody passes the night on deck. The weather is delightful.

Night is over. The sun throws its light over space; then floods in upon the ocean. It is magnificent.

Sunrise is more beautiful here than in Europe.

The waves, the shrouds, and the yards, are painted in brilliant colors. Fire plays within fire. A field of gold spreads out under a dazzling arcade.

The sea is covered with little fishermen's boats. We are now in sight of Nova Scotia.

Soon we arrive at Sandy Hook, and finally we pass Staten Island. The gun of the *Pacific* salutes the Battery, then the fort of the Quarantine.

Here we stop.

The Health Officers come on board.

Before the hospital several steamers of different nations are anchored.

Some have the yellow fever, others the cholera, etc., etc.

In spite of ourselves, we feel uneasy in these quarters. We hold our breath for the few minutes we remain here.

We continue our voyage! and at seven o'clock next morning we enter, under full steam, the bay of New York, which is one of the most beautiful in the world.

Millions of boats, of all sizes and colors, run along delightful shores covered with verdure and flowers.

Finally, we land on the *Pacific's* dock; we leave that horrible box, we press with rapture the soil of the New World, and fall delighted in the arms of Gustave Naquet, minister plenipotentiary of Raphaël to New York; who waits on us to the Custom House, and who seems the least in the world disappointed at seeing us.

That explains itself. They did not expect the *Pacific* for ten hours to come, and a little steamer, chartered to come to meet Mademoiselle Rachel, was to have been filled principally by the Lafayette Guards (the Frenchmen of New York), whose band, on approaching the *Pacific*, would have executed a selection of French airs.

Invitations had been sent out, and gentlemen and even ladies intended to join the Lafayette Guards.

You will appreciate the general disappointment on learning the premature arrival of the *Pacific*. But man proposes, and steam disposes!

And this little aquatic fête fell entirely overboard!

So that she, who was its object, was obliged to land in the imperial city like any common mortal.

She and all her family took carriages and were set down at the St. Nicholas Hotel, very glad, I am sure, to have escaped this serenade, and to have been able to go through the city without being exposed to the impertinent staring of New York loafers.

Unfortunately for her, she had not got rid of this Damoclesian serenade, and, at night when she was sleeping profoundly, the Lafayette Guards collected under her window, and began to play all their repertory.

Bongré, malgré, (willy-nilly), she was compelled to awake, get up, and appear on her balcony.

The Lafayette Guards, satisfied, retired after awhile, and permitted their victim to repose.

She had need of it, and we also!

Third Part.

THE IMPERIAL CITY.

CHAPTER I.

WHICH MAY GIVE AN IDEA OF NEW YORK.

NEW YORK! Here we are!

And not without some trouble; the custom-house officers themselves seemed to oppose our definite entrance to this young capital.

Not a night-cap that they did not inspect; not an unhappy necessity for the voyage that they did not rummage from the top to the bottom.

Ah! here is tit-for-tat, I tell you.

Not a soul, by way of revenge, who was not on the *qui vive* to find out who we were, and if we had our passports all right.

"Who are you? How does it concern you?"

"Your passport?" Eh! what for, bon Dieu! provided you pay the custom-house charges without saying anything, it is all the same thing to them whether one is an honest man or a *gentleman* at large.

American hospitality does not look at one so closely as all that!

She would do well, for instance, some day when she has time, to prevent hackmen on the stand from demanding, for a job of ten minutes, a sum equal to a little more than 46 fr. 75 c.

The following account is correct. There were nine of us in a frightful, yellowish vehicle, in which we were put almost by force, and were made to pay one dollar (5 fr. 25 c.) each, to be taken from the *Pacific* dock to Broome street, about two steps. But what can you expect; there is no tariff in this model country; and if it had pleased the coachman to ask us double or triple, we must have paid it. Charming specimen of American life!

Well, so much the worse for you—why do you take a hackney coach? Can't you go on foot?

Go on foot! That is, unfortunately, almost impossible; look at the paving of this quarter.

Pebbles replace in New York the MacAdam of our city.

When one walks on them, he has every appearance of making a forced march on very hard eggs.

It is insupportably fatiguing to walk even for a single quarter of an hour on these sharp, cutting stones.

One must pass his whole life in balancing himself in these streets, which is tiresome to the last degree.

But, you will say to me, Are there, then, no side-walks?

Oh! yes. There are sometimes even too many; but they are so badly made, that they break and sink down in fifty different places, which form excavations filled with water, which it is not always easy to jump over, without the risk of falling in and getting a little wet.

There is only one thing to be done—the *omnibus!*

Ah! as for that, you have more of those than you want.

In the larger streets, you may see twenty, thirty, forty, abreast; so they are from morning till night perpetual encumbrances.

It is a good thing, however, when you are in a hurry; you are sure with those coaches always to arrive too late.

But as the fare is only six cents and a quarter, you can say nothing.

Besides, these omnibusses are incredibly luxurious in pictures and decorations. Heads of beautiful women, flowers, birds, landscapes, each one more coquettish than the other.

On first arriving, you take all these carriages for perambulating signs of New York glass-painters.

Signs! Of these, one sees all forms and all dimensions.

The houses are literally covered with immense placards.

From the cellar to the garret, you see nothing but high-flown advertisements, colossal canvases, and monstrous bills, all ornamented with huge figures of men having nothing human about them, imaginary animals, and a thousand other representations made solely to draw the simpletons and loafers of the two continents into the shops.

And can you think what all this makes the city look like?

A gigantic hand-bill of a mountebank company.

These are here, also, as well as with us.

Broadway, the *Boulevard des Italiens* of this place, is inundated with them.

Quacks, dentists, breeders of learned dogs, exhibitors of branded negresses, wild beast-tamers, all are in abundance.

One could fancy himself in the fair of an immense village.

What a hubbub! what tumult!

Cries and laughter, songs and oaths; the yells of newsboys mixed with the noise of carriages; the trumpets of charlatans confounded with the bells on the mules who drag eternally on the thousands of railroads which furrow the streets, trains of cars, three feet long, like ours.

Add to all this, carts which get locked together; horses running away; the people one crushes; the loafers to fly from; the drunkards who are being ill-treated, and all the loungers in white vests, who, paraded at the doors of hotels, smoke gravely, their heads down, and their feet in the air; do not forget, above all, the hundreds of prostitutes, with large hands and feet, false teeth, painted cheeks, sunken breasts, who encumber the sidewalks, in the very face of policemen and the sun, and you will have a very small part of the picture which New York presents to the bewildered eyes of the traveller!

CHAPTER II.

IN WHICH EACH ONE TAKES LODGINGS WHERE HE CAN GET THEM.

We have said that Mademoiselle Rachel alighted with her family at the St. Nicholas Hotel.

This hotel, one of the most splendid in the country, is situated in Broadway, of course. (The general rule: Everything is situated in Broadway.)

The front of it is of white marble, *ma foi!* which is truly beautiful; as to the interior, it hasn't the slightest resemblance to our Parisian hotels.

Remember that!

There is everything within (and it is well understood that each thing is to be paid for separately).

Billiard-room, bar, hair-dressing saloon, baths, laundry, etc., etc.

A small city in itself.

There is, even, and not the least curious of all, in this hotel, as well as in several others in New York, an electric telegraph. Do you not think that very convenient, to have only to go down a few steps, to be able to converse, in slippers and dressing-gown, with a friend five or six hundred leagues off?

It is a fact, as curious as authentic (reliable persons have so assured me), that in all these large hotels in the United States, any one can enter the dining-rooms at the hour of repast, seat himself at table, dine, and go away without paying anything. Without paying! Yes, positively! it is strange, but it is so.

It is true that happens very seldom; but when it does, nobody is allowed to demand the least trifle.

You will admit that there is a certain sort of grandeur in this.

I know, of course, that a few dollars more or less is a pitiful consideration for such houses, which are so filled with travellers that there is never a vacant room; but it is, nevertheless, a fact for all that, and I hasten to record it.

There are so many people in this hotel, that

notwithstanding the immense number of waiters, one never knows whom to call upon.

There is a perpetual coming and going, an incessant confusion. The fellows pass their lives in running up stairs and down, from the right to the left, without ever stopping, or scarcely ever obeying the orders given them.

One would think they were stung with the tarantula.

So that it is quite impossible to live in this luxurious caravansary, and as soon as installed one only thinks of one thing: to get out of it as quickly as possible.

Mademoiselle did precisely that. The next day, even, (she lost no time, you see) she, with her two sisters, Lia and Dinah, lived no longer in a hotel (she had had enough of that fantastic existence!), but they took a private house, Clinton place, No. 5.

Raphaël and M. Félix took lodgings somewhere else, in Broadway, if I recollect. (It must have been in Broadway.)

In still another part of the city Mademoiselle Sarah took up her residence.

This division of the Félix family into three

different camps, did not fail to excite the inquisitiveness of all the New York tattlers, who speculated profusely on this subject.

It was, as usual, a much ado about nothing. They lived separately because they lived separately, and that was all.

As to the other members of the *French Company*, the horrible yellow coach, of which I have already spoken, took forcible possession of them on their sortie from the Custom-house, took them—not without jolts, I beg you to believe, and not without very nearly upsetting a number of times—to a certain French-Spanish hotel, kept by a Madame M——.

CHAPTER III.

IN WHICH WE TREAT OF A CERTAIN UNPLEASANT SPECIES OF INSECT.

THE M—— Hotel! Here is another vile place, which it would afford me pleasure *not* to recommend to my friends, if it still existed!

But it is dead! Peace to its ashes!

However, the table there was supplied with French cookery—at least, so they said!

And the best in the city—but they said that everywhere!

Ah! we shall long remember the *côtelettes* that we ate in the house of this worthy woman, and her chocolate à la grease, and her milk à la sheep's brains!

Oh! Desiré! Oh! Verdier! Oh! Vachette! Oh! Bonvalet! Oh! Paris dinners! Where were you?

If we at least had been able to sleep! it would have been a consolation, for,

"*Qui dort, dine.*"

To sleep—ah! well, yes! Under these intemperate latitudes, this function is positively forbidden to Europeans.

Our nights were horrible.

One, among others, was hideous to me. It was the first, *pardieu!*

Towards one o'clock in the morning I awake, a prey to an atrocious itch; I light my candle, and I perceive on my arms, on my legs, on my breast, a whole army of large, reddish crickets, with enormous talons—a kind of insect for which even entomologists, I am sure, have no name, and which Young America has raised up expressly to dissect me!

And these are not all: millions of musquitoes, of all sorts, join the onset, and devour me with unequalled rage.

I feel that my senses are taking leave of me.

I act so, at all events, and I leap out of this too thickly populated bed, and take refuge on a huge trunk, on which I am far from being comfortable.

I swell perceptibly.

Like the serpent Hippolytus, I perceive with horror that my body is but one wound.

Oh! then I curse America, and Christopher Columbus who invented it, and Raphaël Félix who has come to explore it! And I sleep again!

I have a horrible night-mare: I seem to be present at a strange, impossible ball where myriads of fantastic insects have collected together.

Enormous musquitoes, frightful wasps, gigantic crickets, compose the orchestra.

Colossal caterpillars, large hairy spiders, monstrous scorpions, execute nameless quadrilles, and unknown polkas, giddy waltzes, and diabolical rondos, putting to shame the sabbath.

It is the Walpurgis night of the insects!

One hideous spider advances then towards me, and entwining me in her long, thin claws, tries to drag me with her in the whirls of the waltz.

To resist the allurements of this ignoble corypheus, I made such a violent effort that I awoke to see a spider on the calf of one of my legs, breakfasting quietly on the last drops of blood; a real one this time, of a reddish hue, and so like my danseuse of the past night as to be readily taken for her.

This is the way they sleep in this country! travel, then, twelve hundred leagues to enjoy this amusement!

To calm myself, I recollect that to-day is the 284th anniversary of St. Bartholomew.

Indeed, as everybody here is Protestant, these insects, who are of course the same, have avenged on my person, a poor Catholic, that great butchery of the past.

That was right!

CHAPTER IV.

IN WHICH THE MILLION-HUNT BEGINS.

To crown these attractions, it is scarce daybreak when a hand-organ begins to play *les Filles de Marbre* and the *Sire de Franc-Boisy* under my windows.

I thought I had left *those* tunes behind!

Notwithstanding the innumerable wounds of her artistes (for not one of us has been spared by the musquitoes, and as you may well suppose, Mademoiselle Rachel no more than the rest), Raphaël Félix formally announces the first performance of Mademoiselle Rachel and the French company, for the 3rd of September, 1855, in all the newspapers, and that without the least bit of delay.

In fact, we shall soon know what we may count on. Everybody is awaiting, with a curiosity and impatience that are very natural, the issue of this first night, which will indicate very nearly the entire result of the enterprise.

So far, it is starting under excellent auspices.

The press throughout seems to be in the best possible humor.

The *New York Herald*, the *Daily Tribune*, the *Courrier des Etats-Unis*, and twenty other more or less important papers, devote several columns every day to this great literary event, unprecedented in the history of the United States.

The ticket-sale goes on as if it were on rollers.

The administrative money bags are swelling delightfully.

From morning till night, at his office in Wall street (the street which the Millions inhabit!), Raphaël Félix spends his time in exchanging for an enormous amount of dollars a multitude of little pieces of paste-board.

He is in his element there now! And it is a sight to see him, attending to his customers, inscribing all the names on the books, delivering box-orders, packing away money and giving half a dozen employés twenty orders at a time without ever making a mistake.

O potency of the dollar! He who hardly knew a dozen sentences of English when he came on shore here, now finds means to understand this language, which the Americans take special pains to render thoroughly incomprehensible, and what is still harder, he makes himself understood by them!

There is really, in this office in Wall street, a suprising activity.

Ah! it is because from thence proceed all the orders in regard to this great battle which is to be fought so soon.

Expresses scatter all over the city and distribute on their way thousands of programmes, announcing the pieces comprised in the repertory, the names of the actors, etc., etc.

Others take to the journalists their notes of invitation. Gilt-edged notes, *ma foi!* nothing less!

At last the final bills are posted at all the corners of the streets, and the curious and eager crowd has an opportunity to read the following details:

METROPOLITAN THEATRE.

On Monday, Sept. 3rd,

For the first time in this country, M. DE PREMARY'S

new comedy of

LES DROITS DE L'HOMME.

(Same cast as in London.)

After which will be presented Corneille's celebrated tragedy of

LES HORACES.

N. B.—In New York, M. de Prénaray is always called de Prémary. What for?

(Here also same cast as in London.)

Prices of admission to Mademoiselle Rachel's performances:

Orchestra-seats—parquet and parquet-circle,	3 dollars.
First circle, ...	2 dollars.
Upper circle, ...	4 dollars.

Numbered seats may be secured in advance at the above prices, at an extra charge of 25 cents per seat.

As will be seen, the price of seats is much less dear here than in London. We should have supposed quite the contrary.

Seventeen francs for a reserved seat; really that would not be the death of a man.

If the house is not crammed every night with these prices, the New Yorkers will not be willing to come; that is all.

I read in the *Mémoires de Barnum* that *M. John N. Genin* paid in this same city of New York, on the first appearance of Jenny Lind, the colossal sum of 225 dollars for a single seat.

Two hundred and twenty-five dollars! that is to say, eleven hundred and eighty-one francs and twenty-five centimes!

After that, everything is possible.

CHAPTER V.

FIRST NIGHT IN NEW YORK.

On the third of September, therefore, an imposing crowd stood, long before the opening of the doors, in front of the Metropolitan Theatre.

It is understood, of course, that this edifice is, more than anything else, situated in Broadway. It must be!

Over the principal entrance a splendid transparency has been placed, where one can spell in Chinese shadows the following words:

Comédie—Drama—Tragédie.

The name of Rachel has not been forgotten, very properly, and you can see it at your leisure, and as often as you like, on the French and American flags which the New York artist has painted on the upper portion of his transparency, and which you would swear were live flags, they are so well done.

But the mask of tragedy which you see down lower is not so happily imitated. This is something which has not the appearance of being alive! This diabolical face must give all this world a strange idea of tragedy!

Well, never mind, in spite of this caricature —in consequence of it, perhaps—the transparency has an enormous success.

O celebrated transparencies of the *Cosaques* and of the *Prière des Naufragés*, how you are left in the shade, my good friends!

But listen! It is half-past six, and the doors are open!

The crowd begins to invade the theatre! and that too, without cries, without bustle, and almost without speaking.

O Parisian public! thou art not the public to take possession of a theatre in this way!

But Americans are noisy only about their business. In their pleasures they are as tranquil as the late Baptiste.

So every one follows his usher without crowding, and without pushing or incommoding anybody, takes the seat he prefers.

When the stalls are no longer numbered and

reserved, every one has a right to choose the seat he likes best.

Which is very much the best way.

First, because it prevents people who are late from getting good places, and then because it suppresses entirely that tyrannical, venal and morose class of malefactors, who are forever opening boxes, the everlasting plague spot of our Paris theatres!

Meanwhile the spectators have nearly all arrived, and the house already offers a magnificent coup d'œil.

The gentlemen are generally dressed very simply. One thing seems to occasion them a good deal of trouble, they have ripped gloves.

Ah! this is a very gala day for the ladies.

So they are all, with very few exceptions, dressed with an unheard of luxury, and, what is more, an excellent taste.

Not one of them would have been willing to come here to night except in ball-dress; and what ornaments!

There are diamonds by the shovelful, flowers as if it rained flowers.

Not to take into account that they who wear

them are nearly all young, pretty and smiling, and that these pretty republicans have, for the most part, a slightly aristocratic air which is marvellously becoming to them!

They are far better than their husbands, it is due to them to say so much, and as fortunately they are in a majority. Everything is for the best in this best of all possible theatres.

Besides this theatre is really superb and worthy in all respects to receive such fine company.

The green-room is entirely new, ornamented with various and fresh decorations throughout.

Everywhere are very rich carpets, magnificent furniture, and gas burners in all the nooks and corners.

All that has really a pleasant appearance.

But the hour is passing.

The mighty moment approaches!

The orchestra is playing an overture.

A few seconds more and the French company will meet the American public face to face.

At last the green-room clock strikes seven.

The three blows are struck; everybody makes ready; opera glasses are levelled at the stage; the curtain rises; the *Les Droits de l'Homme* is played.

Our friend Jules Prémaray's piece produces an enormous effect, thanks to the numerous Frenchmen who were present at this first performance.

As to the Americans, I dare assert one thing; they did not understand a word of the piece.

As there is no English translation of this play that was the case of course, and we are not surprised at the result.

During these two acts, a time which seems to them two centuries, these good New Yorkers are delightfully bored.

Were it not for the splendid toilettes of the three sisters of Mdlle. Rachel, I am thoroughly convinced that they would be asleep already.

It would be all the same; they are very much vexed at having came so soon and would be glad to give eleven sous to have the thing over.

The French, who trouble themselves very little whether the play amuses these gentlemen of the New World or not, continue to laugh and applaud, nevertheless.

At last the curtain falls, and now the Americans, with the deepest sincerity, join their bravos to those of the French.

It is over! Ouf!

They consent, in concert with our countrymen, to call out all the actors in the comedy, which is considered to be a great thing in this country, where the *claque* is totally unknown.

CHAPTER VI.

IN WHICH MDLLE. RACHEL COMES ON THE SCENE AND JENNY LIND ALSO.

The entr'acte is not long.

Mdlle. Rachel herself is impatient to appear on the scene.

Nevertheless, she is excited, very much excited.

Her hand is icy.

The piece begins.

The public listen religiously to the Alexandrines of Corneille. The most complete silence reigns in the house.

Suddenly a strange, unexpected noise drowns the voices of the actors.

One would say that a frightful storm had come on, and that the rain was furiously beating against all the windows of the house.

Nothing of the kind! The deluge is all in

your eye. The noise is produced merely by innumerable pamphlet copies of *les Horaces*, translated into English, and all the spectators are turning over the leaf together.

Notning can be more comical than to hear this sudden rustling, just in the middle of a passage.

Nothing can be so diverting as the perfect concert in which all these old papers are hustled.

You would say that a regiment in black uniform was executing a military order.

Mdlle. Rachel does not think this so very diverting.

She reflects that these accursed pamphlets are going to cut in two her words, her sentences, and her passages, and that reassures her only partially.

At last, *Sabine* (Mdlle. Durrey) pronounces the line:

" Voyez qu'un bon génie à propos nous l'envoie," etc.

There is a great movement in the house, and Mdlle. Rachel appears.

She is received by three or four salvos of applause: then all becomes perfectly calm and

We avow, frankly, that has satisfied us only very moderately. They ought to have applauded for a whole hour.

Rachel in America! This seems to us something incredible, splendid, wonderful! It was, to our idea, an epoch which ought to revolutionize the whole continent.

Rachel in America! Why, the Indian tribes themselves should have talked it over in their savage forests!

And, instead of that, they receive her just as they have received ten other, twenty other, actresses!

What am I saying! Jenny Lind was received like a queen.

And yet, does Jenny Lind's talent, great as it may be, surpass Rachel's?

I must be permitted to doubt.

As to the reputation of the Swedish songstress, everybody knows that it never was equal to that of the French tragédienne.

But just see what a reception she met with in New York, at the first concert in Castle Garden.

Barnum himself is the narrator:

"One thousand tickets were sold the first day, for an aggregate sum of $10,141 (or 50,705 francs).

"In order to prevent confusion, the doors were opened at five o'clock, although the concert did not commence until eight. The consequence was, that, although five thousand persons were present at the first concert, there was neither accident nor disorder to be deplored. The reception of Jenny Lind, on her first appearance, in point of enthusiasm, was probably never before equalled in the world. When she was led toward the foot-lights, the entire audience *rose to their feet* and welcomed her with three cheers, accompanied by the waving of hats and handkerchiefs. Towards the last portion of the *cavatina*, the audience was so completely carried away by their feelings, that the remainder of the air was completely drowned in a perfect tempest of acclamation, Enthusiasm had been wrought to its highest pitch. Her triumph was complete. At the conclusion of the concert, the songstress was loudly called for, and was obliged to appear three times before the audience could be satisfied."

I should not have repeated here the details of this first night of the Swedish Nightingale, had not fifty persons in New York, on the spot, assured me that all Barnum had said on this subject was strictly true.

It was an incredible infatuation, a rage, a *furore*.

And I repeat it, Rachel's success does not approach that of her predecessor.

All the worse for the Americans.

They appeared to consider it a matter of course, that the French tragédienne should leave her native land and risk her life to have the pleasure of repeating poetry in the country of Washington and Benjamin Franklin. What is worse, they did not understand her.

The things that produced the greatest effect among us, her magnificent diction, the play of her countenance, her admirable carriage and gesture, all these are passed over nearly unnoticed.

The only things which excited real applause, were the strong passages, passionate scenes, where the step becomes more animated, the gesture more lively, or the voice leaves its usual tones.

So the whole of the scene of the imprecations produced a monstrous effect, and decided the effect of the performance, a very brilliant success, very great without doubt, but I would have had it twenty times greater, twenty times more complete, considering the talent and name of her who was its object!

I need not say that Mademoiselle Rachel was called out after the piece, which ended, not at the end, as some may suppose, but two-thirds through the fourth act, that is, at the last words of Camille, when she is slain by her brother: "*Ah, traitre!*" which does not rhyme with any great things.

The scene of Sabine and Horace is suppressed, as is also the fifth act, as injuring the effect.

The public, to do them justice, did not encore anything, and they applauded Rachel as warmly as they could, when, on being called out, she was led on the scene, not, as one would suppose, by her brother *Horace*, but by her brother Raphaël!

Probably because it would not have been proper for Camille to reappear, giving her hand to the man who has just assassinated her!

As you perceive, Mademoiselle Rachel always makes her début in a city in the part of Camille. This is her great *cheval de bataille.*

CHAPTER VII.

IN WHICH IT IS PLAINLY SEEN THAT THE AMERICAN DOES NOT BITE WELL AT TRAGEDY.

One thing is positive, and we all perceived it that night: tragedy is not the least in the world to the American taste.

It is a great deal too serious, a great deal too magisterial, and, above all, a great deal too cold, for them.

All these people, regular business men, (and I do not reproach them for being so,) all these people, I say, are busy all day with their business, their sales, their purchases, their dollars, their thousand things, in fact—every one more tedious than all the rest; and at night, if they consent to shut themselves up in a theatre, they want gay, pleasant spectacles, which divert them a little, and make them forget the labors of the day—pantomimes, comic songs, equestrian scenes, feats of strength, pretty dances and pretty danseuses especially, they ask nothing more.

This explains the immense success and the immense fortune of the Ravels.

Ten times I have been to the Broadway Theatre, of which they are the managers, and I could hardly get a seat, (of course I paid like any one else).

And what did they play? Jocko, or the Brazilian Monkey, and The Devil's Pills, in pantomime; that is all!

Heigho! Raphaël Félix had a presentiment of that when he wanted to engage a corps de ballet!

When I speak of the public of the United States, of course it is understood that I am speaking only of the masses.

There is a class there (unfortunately, it is the minority), but, in short, there is a class who are intelligent, educated, artistic, even; it comprises all the members of the American press.

They have not the everlasting dollar mania in their heads, and they are capable—I can answer for that—of appreciating and judging transatlantic actors and plays.

All the journals have emulated each other in

giving very charming and very remarkable articles on every one of the performances of Mademoiselle Rachel.

The *New York Herald*, among others, has shown the great tragédienne a politeness hitherto unknown.

This journal, printed of course in English, has published, in the midst of its leading articles, criticisms of several of Mademoiselle Rachel's performances, and that, too, in *French*.

Which, certainly, is more than enough to make everybody adopt our opinion of the press of the New World.

The *Courrier des Etats-Unis* (the French journal of New York) has not been behind, as may be supposed, in sustaining the performances of the French Company.

Ah! had the success that was contemplated for this enterprise depended on these gentlemen, I think I do not go too far when I say that it would have been attained as fully as heart could wish; but the public (now it will be understood whom we designate by that name)—the public did not bite at tragedy!

It did not seem to them at all droll to see

actors always coming in, two by two, with their legs too bare and their dresses too short, to declaim great orations long as an endless day.

And then, it completed their stupefaction, to be compelled to follow the piece by these accursed translations. Sometimes they turned over two leaves instead of one, so that it was perfectly impossible for them to make out a single word, and then they went out half crazed!

For a moment, they hoped that these rather slight costumes would have something to do with wrestlers; but alas! they were terribly undeceived!

Gods! what a monstrous success, what frantic bravos, the actor would have obtained, who, in the midst of a tragic scene, had taken to walking on his head, turning summersets, and swallowing his sabre!

And, take notice, that notwithstanding all this, the public have never failed to applaud when they could find an opportunity!

But it was not hearty! it was the applause of politeness, and that was all!

All the grand scenes never affected them seriously.

And the proof of that is, that as soon as an act was over, they never spoke to each other about what they had just been seeing and hearing: no; they began, without losing a minute, to talk about the course of the dollar.

CHAPTER VIII.

IN WHICH THERE IS MORE TALK ABOUT THE SWEDISH NIGHTINGALE.

After the performance was over, we were all perfectly sure that an immense crowd would be in waiting for Mdlle. Rachel at the door of the theatre to carry her in triumph to her house that was to be. Well, instead of that, every spectator hurried as fast as he could to find a place in one of the many omnibusses which take their station every night, when the play is out, in front of the theatres. After which, every one entered his own domicil, absorbed one or two tea-pots of warm water, tucked himself up within his bed-clothes, and went to sleeping tremendously, dreaming of everything but the first night of the French Company in the Metropolitan Theatre.

The receipts for this first night were five thousand six hundred dollars, that is to say, 26,334 francs.

This is evidently very handsome; but what is it in comparison with the *fifty or sixty thousand francs* which we ought to have made?

Above all, what is it in comparison with the receipts of Jenny Lind's first night, which rose to the fabulous sum of 17,864 dollars, that is to say, ninety-three thousand seven hundred and eighty-six francs! And besides—adds Barnum with chagrin—this was not as handsome as it ought to have been, in consequence of some misunderstanding in relation to the sale of the tickets.

There is evidently a difference between these two sums, which would open the eyes of a bat; but there is also, we are perfectly aware, a not less perceptible difference between the two gifts of these two great artists.

Jenny Lind sang, and song is a universal language, which all the world understands; while Rachel plays tragedy. (And this is very far from being a universal language—this tragedy!) Rachel, consequently, could be understood only by the élite of intellect, that is to say, by very few people.

There was, moreover, a still better reason than that why the Rachel receipts never reached the figure of the receipts of the Swedish Nightingale.

This is because, for the Nightingale in question, the seats were sold at auction, by means of which incredible totals were rolled up; while, for Rachel, the seats were sold at the office price, just as in Paris.

So that the Metropolitan Theatre, when completely full, could not have produced an amount of more than *thirty thousand francs.*

Well, in spite of all that, it is our profound conviction that, with the name of Rachel, they should have made thirty-five thousand francs! At the very least?

Yes, the passage-ways should have been crowded, the boxes invaded, in short, spectators should have climbed, per force, upon the shoulders of great good-natured fellows in front of them!

We could have wished to see enthusiasts hanging on the cornices, clinging to the pillars, perched on all the gas-fixtures. We would have had them behind the scenes, on the stage, between the legs of the actors, as in the time of Moliére, when all those people cried:

"*How fine this is!*"—*before the candles were lighted!*

Mdlle. Rachel, too, would have had it so, and Raphaël, and everybody.

However, nobody dared to complain of the result of that first night.

Perhaps they were hoping that, on succeeding nights, the receipts would be handsomer, and the enthusiasm greater.

It was possible!

Amongst other journalists, M. R. de Trobriand, of the *Courrier des Etats-Unis*, came behind the scenes, and congratulated Mdlle. Rachel warmly, assuring her that this night's success must go on increasing.

They believed it! Why should not one have believed it with them?

The next day, September 4th, were played—

PHEDRE AND THE DROITS DE L'HOMME.

(Same cast as in London.)

Strange circumstance! the receipts fell!

Nineteen thousand five hundred and eighty-seven francs are made to-night.

Nearly *seven thousand francs* less than yesterday!

This because they do not understand a word.

The piece, however, produced an enormous effect—greater than *Horace*, perhaps.

Rachel is called out several times, during and after the piece.

The French in New York are enchanted; they applaud frantically.

As to the Americans, they persist in making that disastrous noise with their pamphlets, and in not being amused enormously.

Some of them, who came only to *see* Rachel, leave their seats on her appearance, and hurry away as if the devil were behind them. They have *seen* Rachel! They can say to every body:

"I have seen Rachel."

That is all they want.

As to making a study of the French tragedy and tragédienne, they reserve that pleasure for another time. Meanwhile, they go to the Broadway Theatre to see a certain tight-rope dance, which is making a good deal of noise in the dramatic world of New York.

To-night, through the whole of Rachel's first scene, a number of blackguards, concealed in the passages of the theatre, amuse themselves by imitating the crowing of a cock.

Yesterday, indeed, on her entrée in *Horace*, they were indulging in this barn-yard amusement.

The noise of this fowl, in the midst of the poetry of Corneille and Racine, produced the most disagreeable effect in the world; so they sent in pursuit of this pretended cock a party of policemen, who, of course, found nothing at all.

At the close of this second night, in spite of its success, we were not nearly as well satisfied as we had been the evening before. There was a reason. And we ventured to make the discovery that this country was decidedly too far off, too warm, too full of flies, and not literary enough!

And to think that Raphaël was so obstinate as to undertake this audacious journey.

I made this observation to Mdlle. Rachel.

"What would you have?" she answered; "he cannot be contented anywhere." And she added, with a smile: "My brother, you see, is the Wandering Jew, and I am his five sous."

CHAPTER IX.

IN WHICH WE DON'T PLAY AS MUCH AS WE WOULD LIKE.

On the 6th of September, the bills announced the first performance of *Adrienne*, not *Lecouvreur*, as one would suppose, but of

ADRIENNE *LA*COUVREUR.

(N. B. During the whole time that we were in New York, it was impossible to induce the compositors of the place to call this unfortunate *Adrienne* anything but La*couvreur*—probably, because she was a woman.)

That did not hinder the piece from having a far greater effect than *Phèdre* and *Horace*. Ah! it is because there are such splendid dresses in *Adrienne;* such rich ornaments!

All these ladies play to-night *with all their diamonds!* Mdlle. Sarah is sparkling; Mdlle. Rachel is dazzling. And then, there is a new dress for each act, and it is a great source of pleasure to the spectators no longer to see this eternal palace, eternally decorated with its two old red arm-chairs! Oh! the villainous arm-chairs!

So, with the whole sincerity of their souls, they overwhelm Rachel with recalls and bouquets! She is much greater in this than in *Camille*—than in *Phèdre*, even! So they think! She changes her costume three times, at least! *All right! all right!*

The receipts to-night are 2,026 francs more than yesterday. They ought to be. Next day, they placarded:

MARIE STUART.

But two performances, one immediately after the other, are too much; the sale of tickets gets on slowly.

At this, added to a slight indisposition on the part of Mdlle. Rachel, the word

POSTPONEMENT

takes the opportunity to spread itself magnificently on the bills of the Metropolitan.

Next day, they would have endeavored to make up for this lost night; but fate, disguised as an almanac, willed that it should be Saturday.

Now Saturday, being pretty generally the day before Sunday (even in America!) merchants are obliged to stay very late at their offices, to balance their accounts for the week; and their provident companions spend the evening at market, making provision for the next day; and, for this reason, if there were in every theatre the most attractive and the most gratis spectacles in the world, all these people would rather be chopped as fine as mince meat, than give up their old customs for a single day! Old customs are sacred in *young* America!

For example, the government, seeing with what fury people were rushing into drunkenness, promulgates a law (the Maine Law), prohibiting, throughout the Union, the sale and use of alcoholic drinks. What do they do about it?

They rebel! They jump square-footed over the law; they open the bar-rooms and taverns by force, and the numerous gutters of America are more than ever clogged with drunkards. Their customs, first of all! Apropos of this, at Lincoln, in Illinois, not long ago, the women rebelled, enraged at the intemperance of their husbands. They armed themselves with axes, spades, knives, and even pistols, and took a liquor establishment by assault. Everything was destroyed. The house itself was nearly demolished. *(Historic.)*

Again; some years ago, there was in the United States a very popular game—*the game of nine pins.*

Since colossal sums were lost in this innocent pastime, and every day some player found means to ruin himself out and out, a decree appeared which forbade—this time seriously—*the game of nine pins.*

Straightway there was a great hubbub. No more nine pins! What is to become of us? Must there be another rebellion?

No; upon reflection they discovered, that although *nine* pins were suppressed, there was nothing to hinder them from indulging in a game of *ten* pins.

And, in fact, since then they play at *ten pins* from morning till night. If an ill-advised decree should suppress *ten pins,* they will play at *eleven* pins, and so on, to the extinction of natural heat.

It is a fine thing to cheat the law a little!

So much for the law, *morbleu!* Why does it come poking its nose into their old customs?

CHAPTER X.

WHICH IS VERY FAR FROM BEING A LIVELY ONE.

PERHAPS you think, that because we could not play yesterday, Saturday, we should give at least two performances to-day. No, no. By order, the theatres are closed and the shops are not opened. No cafés, no restaurants! If you did not take precautions yesterday, you are likely to die of hunger to-day.

In the streets there are no hacks; in the dead city a few promenaders, veritable spectres, pass now and then. Not a cry! not a laugh! not even the bark of a stray dog, not even the twitter of a flitting sparrow.

It is exactly so. There are scarcely any dogs in New York; as for swallows, you never see them. Why? It is dismal enough to make a man swallow his own tongue.

Positively, this town is enough to dry one's heart up. All the houses, in white marble or granite, are as like funeral monuments as one drop of water is like another. It is striking; and, in addition to that, each house has its little iron railing enamelled with ivy, cypress and weeping willows.

It is doleful enough all the week; think what it must be on Sunday.

Besides, on this day, every one flies to the country. I, and some of my friends, wish to do like everybody else. So we get into a hack, telling the driver to take us wherever he pleases, so that it be to some very lively place. We start. Presently we are on a kind of bridge, and, in a few seconds, we find that our bridge has left the shore, and that we are in the middle of a river with our carriage and horses. A ride on the water in a coach! That's something like—that's funny!

(This kind of bridge, propelled by steam, is a sort of huge ferry boat—an omnibus boat—big enough to hold hundreds of people, besides some thirty carriages with their horses.)

In a very short time we are on the other side of the river, and our horses drag us into the country. After a rather long ride, we arrive at last at the jolly place chosen by our coachman.

Now, guess where the scamp has brought us? To the graveyard—the Père la Chaise of the place!

Let us leave this Necropolis, and go and take a turn in the Metropolitan Theatre; or rather, not yet. Before leaving the funereal pomps, I have a piece of melancholy news to tell you. The yellow fever is at Norfolk and Portsmouth, and the papers speak of nothing but that.

"While the pestilence seems to diminish at Norfolk," says one of them, "the latest advices from Portsmouth report an increase on that side. If the alarm subsides in the former, it is only to be exacerbated in the latter, city.

"Yesterday we gave the names of some physicians who have died, victims to the disease. To-day we have received a melancholy list of clergymen who have suffered the same fate."

"An association of eleven persons is mentioned—physicians and nurses—who arrived at Portsmouth on the 29th of August, and of whom six perished in a few days afterward.

"It is easy to see that this frightful mortality has made many orphans.

"Interested in the fate of two hundred children thus deprived of their parents, the Baltimore Committee proposed to remove them to the House of Refuge of that city. The ladies now prepared to provide them with new clothes in exchange for their old ones which were burned. But the Howard Association refused to make the transfer, which was relinquished in consequence.

"The dispatches received to-day from Norfolk and Portsmouth," say the journals of the next day, "report no amelioration. Public beneficence is not slower in succoring the victims than the plague in striking them down.

"The subscriptions in New-York alone have reached, up to this time, 25,000 dollars (131,250 francs!) and are increasing every day. The board of Councilmen voted, on Wednesday, the sum of 3,000 dollars.

"At Philadelphia 20,000 dollars have been collected for this noble object. Why is it that one night of frost can do more for the cities thus decimated, than all the sums of money that are sent thither?

"This horrible pestilence falls even in the midst of the sea. Last Sunday some fishermen of Edgartown piloted to this port the schooner Joseph James, of Bangor, which they had found at anchor outside of the Great Rip. The vessel was loaded with pine wood and bound for Georgetown.

"On the voyage, the yellow fever broke out on board with such violence that not a man of the crew escaped. All were on the sick list, unable to work the craft. These unfortunates have been landed at Quarantine and are now the objects of that care which their condition requires."

We read in another journal that Mademoiselle Rachel has sent to the families of the victims the sum of one thousand dollars (5,250 francs).

CHAPTER XI.

IN WHICH THERE IS A GOOD DEAL SAID IN FAVOR OF THE RACHEL COMPANY.

ON Monday the 10th, we play

MARIE STUART.

Leicester, - - - - -	MM.	Randoux.
Mortimer, - - - -	"	Léon Beauvallet.
Melvil, - - - - - -	"	Latouche.
Burleigh, - - - - -	"	Chéry, aîné.
Paulet, - - - - - -	"	Chéry, jeune.
Elizabeth, - - - -	Mdlles.	Sarah.
Marie Stuart, - - - -	"	RACHEL.

Receipts: 20,154 francs—a little less than with *Adrienne.*

Besides, the heat is intolerable. Impossible to dress in anything but white linen.

Which is very expensive, as washing is here ridiculously costly: a single collar *ten sous.*

Wednesday, September 12th.

ADRIENNE ALWAYS *LA* COUVREUR.

Receipts; 18,102 francs.

The *Courrier des Etats-Unis* publishes a very

favorable article on the artists of the *Company Française.*

The article is very long; but as it speaks well of everybody, we shall give the whole of it:

"THE RACHEL COMPANY.

"In hastily committing to paper, on leaving the Metropolitan Theatre, our impressions of each performance, the success of Mademoiselle Rachel has scarcely left us space to say a few words of the manner in which she is supported. The artists who accompany her in her transatlantic tour, deserve, in every respect, a great deal more than this brief notice. We take advantage of our first leisure moment to do them justice.

"At any time, and everywhere, the company with which M. Raphaël Félix has surrounded his sister would be worthy of mention.

"In the United States, accustomed as we are to see the most famous stars appear in the midst of, what is called, in the language of the theatre, a pasteboard troupe, this company exceeds, by a great deal, all that we had a right to expect or require. On this account, it is not alone the appearance of Mademoiselle Rachel which will form an epoch in the dramatic history of the United States. All that is connected with her advent among us, will leave a profound impression in the memory of the public, and, we hope, a germ of regeneration in the customs of the American stage.

"Sublime and startling, certainly, is the revelation of art which Mademoiselle Rachel brings to the New World, in the folds of her tragic robe. But, in a less elevated degree, there is also a revelation in the ensemble and *mise en scène*, which has transformed, for a time, the Metropolitan into an edition of the *Théatre Français*. In this matter the American dramatic world—artists as well as directors—has yet everything to learn; and it will never be able to enjoy a more practical or more eloquent school than that now before its eyes.

"Furthermore, French dramatic art will never achieve a more brilliant triumph than it receives now in New York. Before a people to the greater number of whom our language is unintelligible; before an audience who have never seen any but unnatural effects on the stage, our artists will be heard, understood, and applauded, without modifying a single one of their customs, without having sacrificed a single rule of scenic good taste. They will play in New York as they would play in Paris; and New York will applaud them with the same discernment that Paris would exercise. The instinct of the beautiful, the right, the true, will be correctly appreciated by an audience which understands only the one half.

"No means could be employed to throw out in bolder relief, in a more striking, and at the same time, more flattering, aspect, the degree of perfection which dramatic art has reached with us. But of what a variety of arts, all ignored in the United States, is not this grand art composed! To enter, to go out, to walk, to listen, to look—are so many studies, in which the actor must perfect himself before making any pretensions to merit—before, so to say, even learning to speak. The art of modulating his voice to the diapason of different situations, adding to it proper sentiment and gesture, crowns all the others; but he knows how to supply the place of this, and it is not, so much as it ought to be, the most difficult to acquire. It is the union of all these talents, of all these qualities, from which proceeds the charm, the power, and, above all, the truth, of the scenic art. And the more the whole is dissolved in a sort of natural simplicity, the grander and deeper is the impression produced. It is precisely this which constitutes the distinctive character, and, at the same time, the immense superiority of our theatre; it is this, also, which, at the present moment, causes the success of the Rachel Company, apart from the personal triumphs of the great artiste.

"Assuredly, when an American audience listens with a patient and almost interested ear, to the two long acts of the *Droits de l'Homme;* when it laughs at the discoveries in the last scene of the *Dépit Amoureux;* when it submits, without ennui, to the long explanatory scenes of certain tragedies; when, above all, it applauds spontaneously a moving situation or well-conceived passage, it is not because it has understood all that has been said; but the look, the air, the attitude, the gesture of this actress, have translated the evanescent idea with such fidelity, that the audience almost fancies it has understood the words.

"Moreover, everything is new to him in the play, in the *mise en scène*, of which nothing has sufficed before to give him an idea. These personages, who come and go, depart and reënter, sit down and rise up, in the most natural manner in the world; who walk without measuring the stage with puppet-like steps, and who speak without filling the theatre with jerks of voice; this ease without slovenliness; this action, so expressive, and yet so quiet; this art of filling the stage, not with stride and uproar, but with true action; this historic exactness of gait, physiognomy, and costume—these again are equally the revelations which make an impression, and from which, for that very reason, we have a right to expect a lasting influence.

"The last point to which we allude—historic accuracy—is, certainly, neither the least conspicuous, nor the least important of these revelations. In this respect, more than in all the others, the American theatre is in its infancy—let us say, rather, in chaos. Even upon our best stages, anachronism is a fixture, and artists, the most careful of their parts, approach every instant the grotesque in the matter of dress. Let them study *Phèdre*, *Adrienne Lecouvreur*, *Marie Stuart*, and they will see how a period may be resuscitated, how to evoke from the tomb the characters of the past. One detail will give an idea of the extreme point to which the French theatre pushes its scruples on this score. In the second act of *Adrienne*, Mademoiselle Rachel wears, to represent Roxana in *Bajazet*, not the actual costume of the rôle, but rather the costume in which it was played by Mademoiselle Lecouvreur at the time to which the piece carries us back. It is at the cost of such care that historic truth is attained, and the prestige of the stage rendered legitimate and complete.

"These general observations, which are meant, at the same time, to commend the *ensemble* of the company, have led us further than we wished. But they have their interest, and the artists, of whom we have now to speak, will not find fault with a few lines devoted to their appreciation as individuals.

"The list of feminine *personnel* with which we have been made acquainted, is composed of six names: Mesdemoiselles Sarah, Lia, and Dinah Félix; Mesdemoiselles Durrey and Briard, and Madame Latouche.

"Of the three sisters of Mademoiselle Rachel, Mademoiselle Sarah, up to this time, has been the only one to occupy an important place in the repertory, and she holds it with remarkable talent. The three characters in which we have seen her—as Madame de Lussan, in *Les Droits de l'Homme*, the Duchess de Bouillon, in *Adrienne*, and Queen Elizabeth—have been for her three occasions of complete success. While her piquante grace, her eye full of spirit, and her sarcastic voice, indicate for her the part of the "grande coquette," she has contributed a large share of the most dramatic effects in the last-mentioned plays. Mademoiselle Rachel is admirably posed between her and Mademoiselle Durrey.

"The latter enacts the second tragic parts with as much merit as artistic appreciation. She also, by right, has shared the more striking success of Mademoiselle Rachel. In the Sabine of

Les Horaces, in the Ænone of *Phèdre*, in the Anna of *Marie Stuart*, she has been equally effective. She possesses that gift, so invaluable in her difficult vocation, of being able to put—to use the consecrated term—tears in her voice. She exerts over the audience an influence which has been more than once acknowledged by applause. Mademoiselle Briard plays the ungrateful part of confidante as well as such a part can be played. She showed on Monday night, in the Marinette of the *Le Dépit Amoureux*, that she possesses more intelligence and finesse than can be displayed in the Julies and Irenes of the tragic repertory.

"Mademoiselle Lia Félix sustained very appropriately her part in *Les Droits de l'Homme*, in *Phèdre* (Aricie) and in *Adrienne*. That is all we have to say about her at present.

"Mademoiselle Dinah would be an *ingénue* full of vivacity and very charming, if she would learn from her elder sisters to subdue and modulate her voice, which constantly flies off to the sharpest keys in the juvenile scale. Like her sister Lia, she is yet to be fully appreciated.

"As to Madame Latouche—the only one unmentioned—we caught but a glimpse of her for an instant in the *Dépit Amoureux.*

"MM. Randoux, Léon Beauvallet, the Chérys (father and son), Bellevault, Dieudonné, Latouche, form the masculine part of the *personnel.*

"Almost all of them are already completely ingratiated in the public favor.

"The elder Chéry achieved an excellent success in the Michonnet of *Adrienne Lecouvreur.* M. Bellevault had the same good fortune, and manifested the same talent, in the Duroc of *Les Droits de l'Homme* at first, and afterwards still more completely in the Gros René of the *Dépit Amoureux.*

"The responsibility of the heavy tragic parts rests principally on MM. Randoux and Léon Beauvallet, who both displayed the most valuable and difficult qualities pertaining to this class. M. Randoux, especially, seems to have cultivated tragedy with a care and preference rarely met with now-a-days. We must point out, however, one more error, into which his very love and respect for the majesty of the classics are fast leading him: that is, an extremely slow and tedious delivery. His talent would be improved by burning the board more. M. Léon Beauvallet's acting would also be improved, if he walked better, and did not make the rhyme so perceptible. But it would really be inexcusable for us to criticise artists so unhoped for by us.

"We will add, that M. Léon Beauvallet rendered in a very charming, lively style a rôle in the *Droits de l'Homme*, as foreign as possible to the tragic repertory.

"M. Latouch has appeared before the public in two very different characters: the Prince de Bouillon in *Adrienne Lecouvreur*, and Lord Melvil in *Marie Stuart*. He has put as much good-nature and silly foppery into the first of these characters as true sentiment in the second.

"We will state, finally, that the *jeune premier* of this company, M. Dieudonné, is very happily selected for his parts. *Adrienne Lecouvreur* gave him an opportunity for the creation of a rôle very popular with the public, that of the gallant abbé.

"If, to the personal advantages of each one of the artists whom we have reviewed, be added a remarkable facility in adapting themselves to different styles—an artistic discernment which never is at fault, and a desire to please the audience, which is shown in the most trifling details; if it be taken into consideration, moreover, the manner in which actors of a certain merit support each other, by combining their talents harmoniously together, it will be found that we do not exaggerate in anything, when we present to our readers the company, led by M. Félix, as quite above the common run, and as the most happy combination existing outside the Theatre Français."

CHAPTER XII.

IN WHICH SHOP-KEEPERS AND SAVAGES ARE MENTIONED.

THIS same *Courrier des Etats-Unis*, at whose expense the last chapter was made, and which we are going to put still further under contribution, publishes in its feuilleton the following lines:

"The name of Mademoiselle Rachel figures in all the absurdities of popularity. A Broadway restaurant-keeper has composed the pudding *à la Rachel;* a lady's shoemaker the gaiters *à la Rachel*, "just arrived from Paris;" a confectioner, ices *à la Rachel;* ten wig-makers, the *coiffures à la Rachel.*

"God knows where this emulation of patronage will stop!"

We read, still in the feuilleton of the same journal:

"A grateful fruit-seller has invented the melon *à la Raphaël Félix.*"

"It is not the first time, for that matter, that the New Yorkers have given themselves up to whim. Barnum says, apropos of the Swedish Cantatrice, "We had Jenny Lind gloves, Jenny Lind bonnets and coiffures, anmazons à la Jenny Lind, Jenny Lind shawls, mantillas, skirts, chairs, pianos, Jenny Lind sofas."

I ask you now, what relation there is between Rachel, Jenny Lind, and Raphaël Félix, and this gang of print-sellers, boot-makers, and manufacturers of wigs. But what would you have? Every one must have his catch-word in this country—the grocers and the tinkers of saucepans.

While we are on the shop-keepers of the New World, one word more, if you please. Here these intelligent citizens do not content themselves, as in France, with selling a speciality. Thus the cigar-dealer, for example, sells, indifferently, wine and umbrellas, sweet-meats and clothes, or confectionery. The retail druggist, at the same time with castor oil and seidlitz powders, small glasses of liqueur and some sort of refreshments, sells also chocolate and sponges, burnt almonds and little brushes. The print-dealer sells meat; the butcher, porcelain; the boot-maker, straw hats; the tailor, salt-fish. Here, in trade, everything is allowable, even usury. There are people who sell dollars at two per cent. interest. It's a little dear; but, pshaw! they must make their poor livelihood!

Happily, as the Philadelphia papers inform us, there is actually organized in that city a Company for "personal loans," intended to discharge nearly the same functions as the monts-de-piété in France. "Without awarding to the philanthropy of the shareholders of this Company more, however, than they deserve," says, on this subject, the journal quoted above, "we believe their idea is one, of which the realization may be devoutly wished. The absence of monts-de-piété in the United States, leaves the needy classes at the mercy of pawnbrokers, veritable harpies who devour the substance of the people."

That is really intelligent for so young a people?

Yet there are those who picture to themselves this America as still the primitive country of the old times.

But that America no longer exists; civilization has quite annihilated it.

In these Northern latitudes there is no longer even the shadow of the most attenuated savage, and when, by a miracle of chance, they catch one of the old masters of the new continent, it is in the cage of a station-house that you must go to contemplate him.

Listen to the following story, and you shall see.

"Hi-Kalè-Yow-Matha (which, in any language you like, means "the warrior-with-the-watery-chaps") is the name of a child of the desert, whom the desire to know the world tempted afar from the wigwams of his tribe—so far that, on Saturday morning, my brother, the red-skin, celebrated his arrival in New York, the great city of the pale-faces.

"As the Penobscot warrior is little versed in the modern jurisprudence of the island of Manhattan, and as he ignores, even by name, the temperance law, he thinks he cannot better testify his joy than by copious libations of fire-water. But fire-water is a perfidious fiend to the Indian. Hi-Kalè-Yow-Matha feels, by degrees, his spirits rise from jubilation to martial exaltation; he dreams of deeds of prowess done against the Black Feet, the Choctaws, and the terrible Sioux; he imagines himself marching to the taking of scalps, and he sets about dancing, not without some stumbles, the scalp-dance, with an accompaniment of gestures so wild and yells so warlike, that Sergeant-of-police White thinks it impossible for him to regard the performance otherwise than as disorderly conduct.

"The warrior-of-the-watery-chaps comprehends that his brother, the pale-face, who has a golden star on his breast (in Indian, ki-ke-ha-mi-shuè-ho-hishowioua) would swear an eternal alliance with him against his enemies, so he follows him, without objection, into his palace, to smoke with him the calumet of peace around the council-fire.

"Now the supposed palace was nothing else than the police station, where, without ceremony, they locked up the child of the prairie.

"When, at the sound of the bolts, Hi-Kalè-Yow-Matha perceives the treachery of the pale-face with the heart full of perfidy, he is plunged in gloomy despair. He casts off his garments, one after the other, in token of his grief, and in the state of a child of nature in its simplest expression, he strikes up his death-song; for the prisoner was perfectly free—to sing. He invoked, at first, the souvenirs of his infancy, his sports around the wigwam, the shadows of the woods, the splendor of the sun, the eye of the Great Spirit. Hiawatha could have done no more. But presently the-warrior-of-the-watery-chaps passed to the celebration of his mighty feats of war. He cried, 'The pale-faces have betrayed Hi-Kalè-Yow-Matha! The foxes have coaxed the lion into a trap by licking his feet, and they would devour him. But the lion has claws and terrible teeth, he will pulverize the foxes before he dies. Let them come! Ho! ha! let them come!'

"Then he made such an uproar in the room that the police interfered. On seeing the officers enter, the Indian imagined his enemies were coming to catch him and bind him to the torture-post, and that the time had come for him to crown his glorious life by a death more glorious still. Alone, without arms and without clothes, he threw himself into a fighting attitude, bellowing that they should never scalp him alive.

"The police very judiciously decided that it was nothing more than proper to allow the Penobscot warrior to continue, as long as might suit him, his war-song or his death-song, since it must be called a song. So they closed the door again. Watery-chaps inveighed against his enemies through the key-hole, reproaching them with cowardice, and glorifying his own terrible aspect, which could put to flight an army as countless as the stars in Heaven. Then, little by little, the noise died away. The door was opened softly. Hi-Kalè-Yow-Matha slept the heavy, helpless sleep of a drunken man.

"May the hand of the Great Spirit reconduct the warrior-with-the-watery-chaps back to the wigwam of his fathers." (*Courrier.*)

CHAPTER XIII.

WHICH IS LITTLE ELSE THAN A LETTER TO ROGER DE BEAUVOIR.

SEPTEMBER 14th, sixth night at the Metropolitan,

LES HORACES.

For the second time.

The receipts amounted to 19,293 francs. Which is doing very well for the time of year; and, as the Félix enterprise seemed to be taking a better turn, we take advantage of that to send a statement of our situation.

The statement in question we give here. You will probably recognize some details as having been already mentioned; but you are begged to pay no attention to them. mmn

"NEW YORK, *Sept.* 16th, 1855.

"MY DEAR ROGER:

"I could not come to shake hands with you before my departure for America; allow me to indulge in this exercise across the numerous seas which separate us. Meanwhile, let us talk. What are you doing with that work—you know what? Are you busy on it? I will bet you are not! Try to think a little about it during my absence; if it is not for me, let it be for Porcher. Tell me, is it not so? I will not try to conceal it from you that I shall be happy as several gods to devour a few pages from you. If you knew how little comfort I find in this young America! Fancy, if you can, my dear Roger, that, for nearly a month now that I have been in New York, I have not yet slept a whole night. A portion of my time is devoted to fighting with a cloud of musquitoes, gnats, and other venomous insects, who have selected my hotel for their domicile, and from morning to night are eating me. It is insufferable! I take baths of camphorated alcohol, My room has, at present, the appearance of a branch of the Pharmacie Raspail. These blackguard musquitoes are not content with persecuting me at home, I find them everywhere—in the street, in the country, at the theatre. The other evening, while playing Hippolyte, at the Metropolitan theatre, right in the middle of the declaration in the second act, I was bitten exactly on the end of my nose. You can imagine my perplexing situation. Fortunately, I am told that all this is nothing to New Orleans and Havana, where I am going to be soon. Happy prospect! And to come to this, how many happy moments I spent on board the Pacific. The Pacific! Bitter irony! Ah, my friend, this is the first time that I ever crossed the Atlantic, but I shall remember it! Out of the eleven days which I spent on the vessel in question, I was sick eight at least, living upon ice water and fried potatoes. Those were the only luxuries I could indulge in. So I am thin. Oh, thin enough to throw a rail into desperation. Happily, toward the close of this interesting voyage, I was able to absorb a few bottles of iced champagne. That is the only thing which restored me a little. At last, we doubled Cape Race, after promenading a day in the fogs of Newfoundland (where, by way of parenthesis, I did not see even the tail of one of the dogs of Newfoundland), came merrily into the harbor of New York, in an admirable sunrise, which shed fantastic tints everywhere, and made the colors of the American flag appear still more brilliant. Upon my word, it was superb! Add to that, the guns of the Pacific saluting the Battery and the Quarantine Fort, and you will have the *mise en scène* complete. *Ma foi!* from that moment, I frankly assure you that I have totally forgotten my maritime misadventures.

"At a quarter to eight o'clock in the morning, we set our feet in a cow-stable. This expression is not in exquisite taste, maybe, but I like it—forgive me, I am so camphorated.

"Of course, I shall attempt no description of the city of New York to you. You ought to be as well acquainted with it as I. At any rate, you can consult the Traveller's Guide. It is fine reading—try it.

"One single thing, however, I cannot help telling you; that is, the inmmeasurable number of fires which take place in this capital. It is a hobby, a monomania, a furore—seven, eight, nine, ten a day! It is incredible. In fact, there are so many, that in every house they keep rope-ladders, and other instruments, *ad hoc*. One never goes to bed without a profound conviction that in five minutes the house will be on fire. Meanwhile, fires have passed into one of the customs of the country; it is a habit, a usage. Were there none, people would be disappointed. It is one of the most ardently desired pastimes of the lower classes. And what a tumult when a fire breaks out anywhere! They brawl! They howl! and the alarm sounds, and the bells ring! Really, it is something diabolical! What a droll country! Yesterday, at the St. Nicholas Hotel, two young gentlemen had a dispute. As usual, it ended in stabs. One of them had his belly laid open; he died this morning! What a fine thing it is to talk with these gentlemen! (It appears that the result of this affray has not been so serious; for I have since read in the newspapers, that according to the opinion of the physicians, Capt Wright might be considered to be out of danger. His recovery, which was almost hopeless, after the terrible wounds which he had received in the bar-room of the St. Nicholas, has decided Judge Davidson to admit Messrs. Dean and Montgomery to bail. The two accused had been detained in the Tombs, from the day of the fracas, awaiting the issue of the wounds, to determine their criminality. Both were set at liberty on Saturday, after having given, M. Dean, $5,000 bail as principal, and M. Montgomery, $2,500, as accomplice.) After midnight, assassination thrives in the streets. And they rob! It is incredible. One would hardly believe he was in the New World!

"A good thing about fires: One of my friends, a young man just from France, goes to hire a piano of one of the manufacturers in the city. The price is agreed on; that is all very well; but, after that, guess what this merchant demanded?—that my friend should insure the piano against fire! What do you think of that?

"Another fabulous thing is the price of carriages. On leaving the Pacific's pier, we took a sort of fiacre to go to our hotel. Guess, now, what we paid for it? True, there were nine of us in the fiacre, but it was not more than a ten minutes' drive. We were charged nine dollars—that is to say, forty-five francs. This is a matter of history. What do you say to it? Now, notwithstanding all you may have read in France, about the performances of Rachel in America, I think I must write you a few lines on this subject. You must know, then, first, that Raphaël's plan was very different from that of Barnum in bringing out Jenny Lind. He has not sold the tickets by auction, which has produced a very good effect in the city. As to the matter of receipts, the largest that can possibly be made in Paris is nothing at all by the side of the smallest here. *Horace*, *Adrienne*, *Marie Stuart*, and *Andromaque* have drawn crowded houses. As to the success, I need not say that it has been complete. The American public has received Rachel, and, consequently us also, in very cheering fashion. The whole press has been excellent. In America, at least, one does not have to wait, as with us, until the Monday of every week for an account of a performance. The morning after every important piece, an article appears. And such an article, my friend! Two or three columns at the head of the paper, in the place of honor! Ah! American cities are not so lazy as ours, and in order to write about any considerable performance, they are bravely willing to sit up all night. This is in exquisite taste, and perfectly proper. Is it not true?

"Apropos of critics, say to him of the Patrie, our friend Jules de Prémaray, that his comedy of the *Droits de l'Homme* has already been played three times in New York, with very pretty success. Really, this is not because I play in it; but the piece goes off very well. After the first performance, we were all recalled.

"It is all the same to me, but four months ago, when I brought you the manuscript of our drama, I wish I may be hung if I thought that I should be in the United States now, playing comedy, and tragedy, above all. What a droll thing life is!

"The Lafayette Guards have just addressed a request to Mdlle. Rachel to sing the Marseillaise. She refused, and her letter of refusal was such an amiable one, that these gentlemen really could not feel injured.

"She has just sent to Norfolk a sum of five thousand francs, for the poor devils there who have the yellow fever. Five thousand francs—that does not grow on every bush, as Molière says.

"Sooner or later, I shall probably have played in the United States a grand drama, in five acts, of Lesguillon's and mine; *Washington, or American Independence.* Everybody here thinks that it will make money. I accept the augury. The dollar is good! (The *Washington* in question was never played.)

"Come, I am going to make a trip to Niagara Falls. I will send you a pebble, or something else from there, while you are awaiting the cigars, which I shall forward you from Havana. But I hear the sound of the gong on the stairway. That announces dinner. This is the true moment for closing this missive. (N. B. The tom-tom, or Chinese gong, if you like that better, is used instead of a bell.)

"It reminds me of the fairies of the Cirque, you know, when the evil genius appears. Every time I hear it, I expect to see red flames and a big blackguard of a devil coming to catch me.

"Adieu, dear old fellow, or rather, no, au revoir! Oh! yes! au revoir! Should I say, *au revoir* or *à revoir?* Bah! What odds does it make? But, absolutely, you must write to me, and you must write me an enormous letter, nonsense interminable. I want you to tell me all from over there, all the bon-mots of our friends, all the scandal of our side-scenes. And, as I am not an egotist, I will have your letter published here, so that all the French in New York may share in my good fortune. If anybody asks you for a copy for *Figaro*, and you think well of inserting these notes there, —full liberty.

"*Au* or *à revoir*, then, *my dear.* I grasp all the hands you have. Do not grudge me these two words of English; they are the only English which I know, and I cannot get them off better than in honor of you.

"Ever yours,

"LEON BEAUVALLET.

"New York, United States, viâ England.
"Hotel M——.
"To be forwarded in case of departure."

This letter was in fact publisned in *Figaro*,

and afterwards reproduced in English in the United States. People were furious against me. The unpardonable sin was saying that fires were favorite amusements. However, I am not alone in giving this fact, the *Independence Belge*, among others, is ready to give me a helping hand.

"The pleasure of extinguishing fires," says this journal, "ranks first among amusements in the United States. One must be in the country, and live there a long time, to form a good idea of the American fireman; of his strange passion for fire-engines, which he decorates with flowers, which he embellishes in all possible fashions, and with which he often promenades, for the sole pleasure of showing himself with a pretty engine. No great festival comes off without firemen, and consequently fire-engines; for firemen always take their engines with them. Companies of firemen interchange visits between cities, to show each other their engines, and exchange compliments in relation to them.

"When Alboni arrived in New York, the firemen, apprised of her arrival, were awaiting her upon the dock with their fire-engines. In all industrial exhibitions, fire-engines, of unheard-of magnificence, are to be seen; they have even been made of massive silver. Toy makers manufacture for children little engines, on the model of the large ones. Children play firemen, by setting fire to heaps of paper, or pieces of brush, and then putting it out with their engines, amid the plaudits of all, great and small. The proprietors of tenant houses, partly for the sake of cleanliness, and partly from this inborn taste of every American for fire-engines, rise very early in the morning and throw cold water on the houses, which they wash in this way, as they cannot extinguish them, from the first story to the last." Besides, at the very time when I was writing these notes to Roger de Beauvoir, I learned that in St. John's (New Brunswick), a terrible fire had just destroyed seventeen dwelling houses, with their appurtenances, and in that part of the city known by the name of Vinegar Hill, two other houses and several stables had, in addition, been a prey to the flames in Germaine and Union streets.

As to the mania for assassination in the streets after midnight, which I spoke of in this letter, everybody here has declared that it was false. The fact is, I was wrong in writing "*after midnight.*" There is just as much assassination before.

And this exercise is not confined to men alone, the very women indulge in it here with success.

In proof, a citizen of the place, Thomas Carey, was found one night, about half-past nine, lying on the side-walk in Park Place. He had been attacked by a band of unfortunate females, who had maltreated him so cruelly that the poor devil had to be taken to the hospital.

What a funny world!

CHAPTER XIV.

IN WHICH THE MILLION-HUNT IS FURIOUSLY CONTINUED.

On the fifteenth of September was placarded,

PHEDRE AND THE DROITS DE L'HOMME.

For the second time there is a postponement. Mdlle. Lia is indisposed and the audience does not promise to be very large.

On the seventeenth of September, the seventh night,

ANDROMAQUE AND THE DROITS DE L'HOMME.

Receipts, 18,469 francs.

On the 19th of September, the eighth night,

LA LIGNE DROIT AND ANGELO.

CAST.

Angelo, ...	MM. Latouche.
Homodei, ...	Chery, aîné.
Rodolpho, ...	Randoux.
Catarina, ...	Mlles. Lia Felix.
La Tisbe, ...	RACHEL.

Same receipts as day before yesterday.

The piece obtains a colossal success. Recall, flowers. It lacks nothing.

Drama pleases Americans decidedly.

On the 20th, the ninth night,

BAJAZET.

CAST.

Bajazet,	MM.	Léon Beauvallet.
Acomat,		Chery, aîné.
Atalide,	Mdlles.	Lia.
Roxane,		RACHEL.

Receipts, 18,401 francs.

Although this evening's receipts are nearly the same as yesterday's, the house has the appearance of being not nearly as full. The reason is, that all the free list were present at the drama of Victor Hugo, and that they do not care to see the celebrated tragedy of Racine!

So how solemn it is to-night. One would imagine that to-day was Sunday. When Mademoiselle Rachel is not on the scene the audience show no interest. During the long scenes of Bajazet and Atalide, even the orchestra quietly leave their places, and file out one after the other by the orchestra door. But the administration saw them deserting and compelled them to listen to Bajazet, under penalty of a fine. This argument brings them back to the orchestra and their duty. They endeavor in vain to listen. Sleep takes possession of them, and soon formidable snores are resounding here and there. The noise even of the pamphlets diminishes little by little. One can perceive that sleep is gaining ground. But if Racine's tragedy meets with a rather chilling success tonight, it is because the Americans are such lovers of Russia that they can have no sort of sympathy with a piece so Turkish as Bajazet!

Be that as it may, an orchestra stall, as wide awake as a pot full of mice, *ma foi!* follows the piece by an English translation which it has purchased. It has been there ever since the beginning of the performance, and it has been reading its translation ever since the curtain rose. Unfortunately before *Bajazet*, *Le Mari de la Veuve* is played. The orchestra stall was ignorant of this little detail, and, as it has only come for Rachel, never dreams for an instant that it is possible to play anything but one of Rachel's pieces, and follows the petite comedy by studying the first act of Bajazet. The tragedy is commenced, the stall sees people disguised as Turks, thinks that it may be a masked ball, and, without troubling its head further about this change of costume, follows the first act by the second of the translation, the second by the third, the third by the fourth, and the fourth by the fifth! So that, when we began the last act, the stall had finished its translation.

Oh, then, it completely lost its self-control. It stared at us a few moments with haggard eyes, then seizing its hat, it ran away, waking up everybody upon its path.

On Monday, the 24th, the tenth night,

ANGELO.

In compliance with the frequently-expressed desire of the press and the public of New York, the management reduces the price of certain places.

The parquet, the parquet circle, and the first circle now cost two dollars.

The gallery costs no more than fifty cents.

And, finally, numbered and reserved seats can be secured, without paying a sou more.

Notwithstanding this important decrease, or,

rather, in consequence of it, since it is that which has been asked for, 3,646 dollars are made to night! (19,141 francs.)

Which proves that Americans, who make so much money, prefer keeping it to spending it for their amusement. I was very far from supposing that! One thing I was a hundred leagues further from supposing: a gentleman followed the whole piece of Angelo on the translation of *Marie Stuart* (historic).

On Tuesday, the 25th, eleventh night,

READING,

given by Mdlle. Rachel, at the Broadway Tabernacle.

Mdlle. Rachel gives one act of *Esther*, one act of *Athalie*, one act of the *Misanthrope*, and one act of *Phèdre*.

This is a charming little entertainment. For the moderate sum of one dollar and a half, all the world can come. Unhappily, all the world does not come.

The receipts are not at all good, and, as Mdlle. Rachel gets her 6,000 francs all the same, it is a bad speculation. Mdlle. Rachel, in view of this result, proposes to her manager that she will give a second night similar to this. It will make but little difference. She will not take her 6,000 francs!

Accepted unanimously!

It is a horrible thing, moreover, to recite tragic Alexandrines in a black dress, and especially to recite them in a sort of church, where you feel so uncomfortable, stuck up, as you are, on a narrow platform. It gives you the appearance of being in the little play-room of a *café chantant.* This kind of exercise is unpleasant to the last degree.

CHAPTER XV.

WHICH CONTAINS THE HISTORY OF THE MARSEILLAISE IN THE UNITED STATES.

On the 26th of September is given—

PHEDRE. LA LIGNE DROITE.

Receipts, 16,920 francs.

For the last dozen days, the French in New York, principally the Lafayette Guard, have spent a good part of their time in entreating Mdlle. Rachel to give the *Marseillaise.*

Again and again! Mdlle. Rachel has refused up to this time persistently! But the Lafayette Guards do not give it up so, and, this very evening, they are going to give her, after the play, a superb serenade; after which, she will be obliged to acquiesce in their wishes.

This bit of news circulates among the audience; and, after *Phèdre,* everybody rushes to Mdlle. Rachel's residence, to see the sight.

O, deep deception! O, departed joy! So

much cold water was thrown on the serenade, that there was none. And, when I speak of cold water, I speak literally. The weather is horrid—a perfect flood, enough to wash away the deluge! The musicians were at their post; but the storm scattered everything! In the gutters, now swelled into rivers, flageolets and double-basses were seen floating at the mercy of the waters!

You may think, perhaps, that the Lafayette Guards have abandoned their project. Ah! very well! On the second day but one after the performance of

MORE ADRIENNE AND MORE LACOUVREUR,

the band of the Lafayette Guards takes its place before the windows of Mdlle. Rachel, who is just then taking supper with her family.

The serenade commences. People rush up from all sides. At the conclusion of this outdoor concert, there is a furious cry of *La Marseillaise!*

The musicians play the *Marseillaise.* After the execution of this patriotic air, the cry rises still more furiously, *La Marseillaise! La Marseillaise!*

This time it is addressed to Mdlle. Rachel. A long pause. Nobody appears at the balcony. The blinds are still closed. Murmurs in the crowd. Another long pause. At last the blinds open. Rachel makes her appearance at the window. Cheers by the crowd. The musicians take advantage of that to recommence the *Marseillaise*, and to play a snatch of the national air of the Yankees. Mdlle. Rachel rises.

Ah! she is going to speak! Bravo! Mistake! Immediately on rising, she leaves the window, and the servant gravely closes the blinds, to the great dismay of the crowd and the musicians. Another long pause, and not a few murmurs. They are very much vexed.

But, O surprise! Raphaël Félix, the manager, appears on the steps. Whispers are hushed, hope is renewed, and they listen eagerly to the ambassador of the grand tragédienne.

Here is his speech—but, no, his speech I will not give you, for I have forgotten it. All that I remember is, that he promised solemnly that at an early performance Mdlle. Rachel should sing this famous *Marseillaise* of which they are in such pressing need.

People are comforted, and indulge in prolonged acclamations on their way home.

As for me, I call on the queen of the fête to congratulate her on this nocturnal worship.

At first, I am not recognized, and I am prevented from penetrating into the sanctuary of Melpomene, I do not know why.

Mdlle. Rachel, I am told, has been so much excited by this musical scene, that she is indisposed just at present, and cannot receive!

But I give my name and surname, I enter, and I perceive, thank God, that Mdlle. Rachel is not so indisposed as I feared, for I find her with her family and an excellent appetite in the act of finishing the not less excellent supper which the Lafayette Guard Band had so patriotically interrupted.

This supper, excellent as it was, did not prevent Raphaël Félix from giving, on the next Sunday, to his artists and several editors, a grand dinner in honor of his birth-day, at the Delmonico Restaurant. We are very merry all round. Mdlle. Rachel herself, contrary to her custom, ventures to sing a little. Not the *Marseillaise*. Oh, no! Only Levassor's little song:

"C'est bon'homme qu'on me nomme!"

Altogether, everybody is in marvellous good-humor, and numerous toasts are given to *America*, to the *Rachel enterprise*, and especially to the *Capture of Sebastopol!* for the steamship *Africa* brought us this immense news three days ago!

The day after this managerial fête

ANDROMAQUE

is played. Every day is not a gala day. The promise of the *Marseillaise* injures the receipts immensely; they amount to but 12,211 francs. They have never been so small! Another thing, which is still worse, is, that Mdlle. Rachel catches cold in the side-scenes and is very hoarse. It is very cold now in New York; the nights are freezing. On the 3d of October POLYEUCTE is given.

The receipts are but little better than at the last performance, 2,625 dollars, that is to say,

13,781 poor francs and 25 miserable centimes! On the 5th, ANGELO does better. The receipts rise to 17,335 francs. That is very fair.

At last the great day has come, and on the 8th the bill is proud to announce to the world the following programme:

LE CHAPEAU D'UN HORLOGER.

HORACE AND LA MARSEILLAISE!

Free tickets generally suspended with the exception of the press.—La Marseillaise!

The Lafayette Guards have attained their object. There was a great cry in Paris against these poor Americans, and if a single one of them had dreamed for an instant of calling for the song of Rouget de l'Isle, we should have been very much astonished! They came to hear her and that is the whole of it; they came in pretty good numbers, too, for the receipts to-night amount to 21,299 francs. What shall I say to you about the *Marseillaise* as sung by Mdlle. Rachel? Everybody has heard it, and can only assert one thing; it produced a greater effect in Paris than it did in New York. There is not so much enthusiasm as was expected, which was proved after an intercalatory performance of

MARIE STUART,

(receipts 14,299 francs, 25 centimes). When this same

MARSEILLAISE WITH POLYEUCTE

was given for the second time, the receipts amounted to the (comparatively) very moderate sum of 15,267 francs. That night, however, Raphaël makes his début in the New World, he playing Polyeucte. These Americans have no respect for anything!

I pass over, in silence, a second reading in Niblo's Saloon, which is not much more brilliant than the first, and come immediately to the benefit night of Mdlle. Rachel.

JEANNE D'ARC,

is played for this time only, the grand aria of

I PURITANI

is sung by Mme A. de La Grange, and finally

LA MARSEILLAISE

is sung for the third and last time. The price of tickets is raised. Proscenium boxes 32 dollars; (160 francs)! Parquette, ·3 dollars; First Circle, 2 dollars; Gallery, 50 cents, as usual. The receipts are 22,128 francs. Mdlle. Rachel is very much fatigued this evening. She has a cold in her chest from which she suffers severely. In spite of that, she is in such a hurry to have done with America that from this time forth she plays every night.

On the 17th, ADRIENNE, 18,228 francs.

On the 18th, PHEDRE and LE MOINEAU DE LESBIE, 19,813 francs.

On the 19th, ADRIENNE again, 18,102 francs.

And finally on the 20th, HORACE and the second act of the MISANTHROPE, 16,259 francs.

This last night, the printer amuses himself with printing on the bill "for the benefit of the artists." It was nothing but pleasantry, and had no sort of effect. To close accounts with the Metropolitan Theatre, which we shall see no more, we will say that M. Raphaël leased it at 600 dollars a night, 3,150 francs! It was not paid!

But I hear, at the corner of Canal street, the locomotive muttering! The bell calls us! Boston is awaiting us! Quick.

To the car and the road for the New Athens!

Fourth Part.

THE MODERN ATHENS.

CHAPTER I.

IN WHICH WE GET A TASTE OF AMERICAN RAILROADS.

WITH gold, one can get over anything, even an American Sunday. So, in spite of the law which forbids the use of any sort of railroad on this too holy day, we are able, thanks to a pretty collection of portraits of liberty, to get in the special mail train, and leave New York with all the rapidity of—mules.

Mon Dieu, yes, mules, nothing else!

Steam will not come yet awhile—but it will come!

They had told us all sorts of horrible stories about American railroads, and as, after all, none of us had even a limb broken, we should be ungrateful to complain ; but it is all the same, when you come out of it safe and sound, you can only say that fate has greatly favored you.

It is quite inconceivable how few precautions are taken to avert accidents.

The rails are laid down alike, on the roads, in streets, and in the very midst of towns.

You would imagine that there would be, at least, railings, or some sort of barriers. Bah! How could Americans take time to think of such fooleries?

So long as the train is drawn by mules, it is all very well; but when steam is put on, and it flies like lightning through streets and public squares, without even a banister to prevent promenaders or animals from being ground under the wheels of the furious engine, the only wonder is that there are not a great many more accidents.

When going through a street or a village, they ring a bell, and that is all. So much the worse for those who are deaf!

Another folly in this country is to have only one track; which is charming, because when two trains rush upon each other, one of them is sure of being finished; but they are in such a hurry—these sons of the New World!

To have made two tracks would have taken twice the time, and wouldn't have answered. It might, perhaps, have saved the lives of several thousand persons! *Fudge!* what is the life of a man worth in this country?

They care for one thing only, to do quickly what they do at all.

So in looking at the streets, which they scarcely give themselves time to pave with pebbles; sidewalks so hastily constructed, that on the morrow they are broken in fifty places; houses that are built in a day—real card-castles that a strong wind will blow down;—and, to return to our subject, fantastic railroads, manufactured to please the devil, thrown across rivers, over quicksands, one is very apt to think that this people, who are there by accident after all, has very little faith itself, even in its own existence, and that it hurries to make the best of its time.

Ah! it is evident that steam was invented for its use. Everywhere, on every corner you hear it at work. They build by steam; they make bread by steam; they wash by steam; eat by steam; execute works of art by steam; they do everything by steam!

They really look as if they were convinced that, from one moment to another, a great flood is on the point of engulfing them and their America in the abyss of the sea which growls around their cities, and seems to be waiting its prey. "To be sure, it never occurs to any one to deny the immense advantages which civilization owes to the discovery of steam. In this matter there is no country which has profited more by it than the United States. But every shield has its other side, and here is the melancholy proof of it: *Lloyd's Steamboat Directory* informs us that since its introduction in the navigation of the western waters, steam has cost 39,672 lives, and 381 boats, with their cargoes. All amounting to a sum of $867,000,000. We do not know the precise date when this frightful list was closed, but everybody knows that, unfortunately, the account is always open to new entries."—*Courrier.*

CHAPTER II.

WHICH TREATS OF ELECTIONS AND SQUIRRELS.

MADEMOISELLE RACHEL leaves with all her company. Her cold does not seem inclined to part with her, for she coughs frequently during the trip. These little excursions do nothing towards curing her—although they are made with all the comfort possible.

We have a reserved car, in which no stranger is admitted. Here, although we expect a running-off-the-track, or some accident more or less disagreeable, we none the less regale ourselves with a light supper of truffles and champagne, which shortens the journey a little.

Our car is immense ; it could easily accommodate fifty people.

Unhappily there is in this great box a stove, which smokes nearly all the time, and seats with backs which are of just such a height as to prevent us from resting our heads, and sleeping a little.

So we are not sorry to arrive, at three o'clock in the morning, in the famous city of Boston, the puritan city *par excellence*, dignified by its inhabitants with the name of *The Modern Athens.*

Mademoiselle Rachel and her family stop at the Tremont House; the Company at A——s' Hotel—a very dear, badly-kept house, and the table utterly intolerable. Unadulterated American cookery. Everything served at once on the table. Because it happens to be as cold as Greenland, it is impossible to get anything warm to eat! The bread is baked just as you go to dinner, and is burning when brought to you, and, moreover, it is very much like a ball of starch. Another agreeable thing is, that this is a *temperance* hotel, and no means of getting even the smallest bottle of Bordeaux.

It is scarcely necessary to say, that we took other lodgings the next day—with a Frenchman, *ma foi!* a brave Bourguignon, who gave us pretty good wine, and a table rather more decent, but who abused our good-nature somewhat with ragoûts of squirrels.

Ah! he made us swallow squirrel! It is frightful! I should never have believed that

Boston could produce so many of these little long-tailed animals!

And I have always suspected that, occasionally, his ragoût of squirrels was nothing but a fricassée of rats!

Eh! *mon Dieu*, are they not both quadrupeds of the gnawing order? Are they not both equally disagreeable? For the rest, what does it matter?

Notwithstanding its squirrel peculiarity, the modern Athens is, none the less, a rather handsome city. Not exceedingly gay; oh! no, on the contrary, very sad!

Happily we came during a holiday occasion, a sort of agricultural meeting, which had attracted a good many strangers.

It is, besides, election time, and that amused us not a little. The elections of '48 were nothing compared to these! What a host of placards, letters, bulletins, bills, and catchwords! The naïveté of the candidates is truly admirable, in having their portraits painted in distemper, on huge transparencies, to captivate the voters. Do you understand that? Their portraits!

In all the streets, ropes are extended from one house to the other, and on these, swinging gently the heads of the future representatives, much larger than nature. When you see all these the sport of the wind, you would imagine yourself present at the *Ballet des grosses têtes* (on the hangman's rope). It is very funny! But what is less so, is the deplorable custom which prevails in the United States during the elections, of conversing too often with a knife or a revolver in hand. From time to time one reads in the journal—

"M. X. . . . was buried this morning. He received yesterday, *by accident*, a ball in his chest."

And that is all. They take good care not to add, "the law will take the case in hand." Fine business truly for justice, one ball, more or less, in a man's chest. Let it stay there!

For instance: "On the night of the election (in New York), a political procession was passing through Tenth street, when a pistol shot was heard. M. John Martin, living in Eighth street, No. 317, fell instantly, in the ranks, struck by a ball in the thigh. He was immediately carried to his dwelling, where the ball was extracted; but the wound having afterwards presented very serious signs of inflammation, M. John Martin was taken to a private hospital. What is strangest in the affair is, that the culprit has not yet been arrested."—*Courrier des Etats-Unis.*

On the other hand, even if the bungler had been arrested who had committed murder *accidentally*, he would only have had to give bail, and that would have been the end of it.

Dollars! always dollars! With them one can get over all these little fantasies under the beautiful sky of America! So much the worse for the poor, and *vive la liberté!*

CHAPTER III.

IN WHICH WE GLANCE AT THE MODERN ATHENS.

If to use the revolver, when one pleases, in revenge, is permitted in the United States, in Boston you are forbidden to smoke or spit in the streets. You never see a Bostonian indulging in this sort of recreation in the streets of his capital.

For instance: a Frenchman could not go out without having a cigar in his mouth, and I ought to do the policemen the justice to say that, when they saw foreigners disobeying the law, they had the good taste to say nothing, but let them continue their Havana in all liberty.

These policemen are, moreover, very polite and obliging.

Not satisfied with pointing out to you the street you are looking for, they often give themselves the trouble to conduct you there; when a long line of vehicles keeps you from crossing, they raise their bâton, and the carriages stop, to let you pass.

Would that the police in every country were like this!

To sum up, the capital of Massachusetts is not wanting in honors or fine traditions.

Hence marched the militia who first fought the English in the cause of liberty.

Here Franklin was born (you may, to this day, see the spot where was formerly the little shop in which, a little child, he made—candles).

On the heights which overlook the city, the famous battle of Bunker Hill took place.

Here, finally, was published, in 1764, the first journal which was issued in the colonies. (Seventy years later, in 1834, there were, in the same city, one hundred and eight newspapers!) (*Annual Almanac for* 1855.)

There are, besides, some fine monuments in Boston; and a magnificent harbor. This latter has but one defect—it is strewn with dried codfish, which has not a very delightful odor.

While we were in raptures over this great quantity of deceased fish, three persons, who were there, commenced, unasked, to give us some details concerning the codfish trade.

These kind people, who, from their accent, we took for natives of Lower Normandy, closed by telling us that Canada was the country in which they first saw the light; where, notwithstanding the English rule, they persisted in speaking French, as before—that is, the true low-Normandy patois.

Why this patois more than any other? one may ask.

That is one of the many mysteries of this mysterious country.

They say it is because there are abundance of apples in Canada, and because this fruit is equally the pride of Normandy; but they cannot prove it. But it is certain that the Canadians speak Norman patois!

Let us go on!

In the window of a book store, not far from the harbor, I read, with a sort of interest, the following programme (Why was it there?—I cannot guess):

HOLIDAY STREET THEATRE.

(Baltimore.)

To commence with the great play, translated from the French of ALEXANDRE DUMAS, expressly for MISS INCE.

CAMILLE.

LE DAME AUX CAMILLIAS!

This piece has been performed in all the American theatres, and has everywhere met with the greatest success. There is nothing astonishing in that, because it is an exact translation of the remarkable work of Alexandre Dumas (son). Here, as it appears, the play is by Dumas (father). The name of Marguerite Gautier was replaced by that of CAMILLE. You will laugh when you learn why. *Camellia,* in English, is written Camillia, and the translator thought it fine to profit by this orthography, and call the Lady of the Camelias: Camille.—"Camille, Camillias." A charming play upon words. Who will say now that the Americans do not cultivate puns?

CHAPTER IV.

IN WHICH IT IS SHOWN THAT BOSTON IS A LITERARY CITY.

While we are exploring the puritan city, the ticket office, every minute in the day, is as full as an egg. The receipts will be beautiful. In fact, at the Grand Theatre, this evening, are played

LES HORACES AND LE CHAPEAU D'UN HORLOGER,

and 19,855 francs are taken.

The audience is admirably composed, better than at New York.

Boston is a very rich and very aristocratic city. The toilettes are splendid, the diamonds innumerable; and this time, a long line of private carriages is drawn up before the theatre, which is evidently one of the finest, if not the very finest, in the whole world.

The house is immense and well arranged—not a bad place in it; and the whole is decorated with surpassing luxury.

In all the galleries are superb carpets, and vases filled with exotics.

The saloons, the lobbies, furnished in the latest fashion; the hangings and upholstery in the best style, and everywhere oceans of light. It is wonderful!

The stage and the wings are no less beautiful.

Here the decorations are magnificent, the accessories profuse. At this very time they are engaged in getting up Macbeth in splendid style, for the engagement of Forrest, who is going to play at the *Boston Theatre* soon after Rachel.

This Forrest is the American Frederick Lemaitre. He has a colossal reputation and furious successes. He is not engaged in any theatre, but plays in all the cities for the moderate sum of four hundred dollars (two thousand one hundred francs) a night.

It is this same Forrest who formerly performed in England, and who was received in such a frightful manner.

Forrest pretended that it was Macready who laid the plot.

So that, when the English tragedian came to New York to play, he was literally hooted.

Forrest made a terrible row. The whole city took part in the quarrel.

The evening of Macready's first appearance, there was a fight in the house. The city guard interfered. Many musket shots were fired, and more than one person was buried next day. Delightful country!

In spite of his great popularity, Forrest has been compelled to settle fifteen thousand francs on his wife, from whom he has been legally separated.

It is even more than a separation—it is a divorce; and a very strange one, for only the wife has the right to marry again.

As for him, he is entirely acquitted of all blame. Such funny laws!

To return to the performance of *Horaces*, we should say that the effect produced by Mademoiselle Rachel was very great, and the success immense. Next day,

PHEDRE AND LE DEPIT

were played.

19,561 francs were taken in.

On the 24th, the first time of

ANGELO.

Here everything is exactly the opposite of New York. They like tragedy better than drama, and Hugo's play drew only 17,834 francs. Boston is the literary city of the Union.

Again, on the 25th, with

ANDROMAQUE,

the enormous sum of 20,559 francs is taken. The impression is more and more complete. Soon after the tragedy everybody rushes out, banging the box-doors with an outrageous noise, and without even the appearance of dreaming the least in the world that *la Mari de la Veuve* is about to be played.

On the 26th, 17,997 francs were taken in for Lebrun's tragedy of

MARIE STUART.

The receipts are so reducing that we run the risk of playing next day, the 27th, although it is Saturday! That is daring! But *aut*—I was just going to make a Latin quotation. Reckless!

This affair is certainly the prettiest in which we have yet been concerned.

ADRIENNE LECOUVREUR

was played to the diamonds.

The performance commenced at three o'clock in the afternoon. At this hour, especially on Saturday, all Americans are shut up in their offices making their payments for the week. So, what happens? Nothing but that there are only women in the house. Not a masculine face or dress disfigures the bewildering charm of the *ensemble*. It is truly an adorable thing to see such a beautiful theatre overflowing with charming ladies (the ladies are generally charming in Boston!) in ball-dresses, bare heads and shoulders, resplendent with gems and flowers.

Receipts, 16,873 francs; which is prodigious for a Saturday.

The performance is over at eight o'clock precisely. Only to think that it is not three o'clock in Paris! What a strange thing! When it is midnight here, it will be striking seven over there. In Boston we shall have been in bed this long time, when the Parisian Theatres have only just opened their doors. The truth is, we are five hours behindhand in this New World—that's just it! If there were an electric telegraph between the two continents, the American news would arrive in Europe five hours before it was sent. That would be so original.

CHAPTER V.

IN WHICH THE PRESS BEGINS TO SHOW ITS TEETH.

THE receipts from Adrienne naturally gave rise to the expectation that, with

POLYEUCTE AND LE MOINEAU DE LESBIE,

(Rachel in two pieces), we should make a prodigious quantity of money!

So we were profoundly dejected, when we saw an almost empty house, and the receipts only four thousand two hundred francs.

What does it mean? There is something under all this, evidently.

In fact, there are furious articles in almost all the city papers. But why? why? What the devil have we done to the journalists?

The report runs that we have given them ineligible seats; and that this somewhat cavalier fashion of treating the press has exasperated them to the last degree. Besides, the journals find fault with another thing, and that is, that, in some places, the seats are sold at a price higher than that named in the bills, and they fiercely charge the management with speculation in this matter, as if the management could help it.

One journal among others is so irritated, that it prints at length the following anecdote :— An apothecary in Boston had displayed before his door a jar with the label *Sangsues* d'Europe. A *gentleman* enters and asks the astonished apothecary for two tickets for the next performance of the French company. The apothecary replies, that he does not keep that sort of physic, and that the ticket-office is a little further on. "*Oh! pardon*, sir," rejoins the *gentleman*, bowing; "but you have at your door *sangsues d'Europe* (European leeches), and I naturally supposed that this was the office of the Rachel company."

M. Raphaël Félix easily satisfied these gentlemen of the press that he was completely a stranger to the speculation which had so irritated them; and on Thursday, November 1st,

ADRIENNE LECOUVREUR

was played for the second time before 15,960 francs. The storm was laid. Ah! the press is everything in America. So much the worse for those who get wet!

While Mademoiselle Rachel is playing *Adrienne Lecouvreur* at the *Boston Theatre*, "the eminent American actress," Miss Eliza Logan, is playing, at the *Boston Museum*, ADRIENNE, or THE YOUTH OF THE MARSHAL DE SAXE, translated from M. Scribe's piece. (They play nothing but translations here.)

In the English translation, *le Prince de Bouillon* is called *the Duke d'Aumont*, and *the princess* is no other than his lady-love. American modesty is offended at seeing *Madame de Bouillon*, who is married, the mistress of the *Count de Saxe;* but finds it all very natural that the same woman should have a lover on the eve of her marriage with the *Duke d'Aumont*. Certainly these are sharp scruples; and in this country they have a queer way of explaining morals. Nevertheless, it is so! They deny that a married woman may behave badly; but as for the young girls, they may do whatever enters their heads, and no one must say a word.

We must not permit ourselves to judge the American artists, whose language we do not understand. All we can say about them is, that they produce an enormous effect on their own public. *Miss Eliza Logan*, *Mr. Keach*, and *Mr. W. Warren*, all three enjoy a prodigious success. *Mr. W. Warren*, who plays in the rôle of *Michonnet*, has seemed to me exceedingly remarkable. He renders the part of the old stage-manager with veritable talent, and I have applauded him with the whole house.

One thing that we cannot pass by in silence is, the wretched manner in which they are costumed. In *Adrienne* they have accoutrements which belong to no period or style, and which have not even the poor advantage of being pretty (I do not allude to Mr. Warren, who was irreproachably costumed)—and, besides, in this piece some of them play with powdered perukes, and others with their hair coiffed à la Louis XVIII.

The artist who plays the *Abbé de Chazeuil* sports, in spite of his powder, an enormous pair of black whiskers. A Louis-XV. abbé, adorned with cutlets *à l'Anglaise*, is a little rash. But what would you have? Nobody takes the trouble to give them good advice. Is it their fault?

CHAPTER VI.

IN WHICH WE PART FROM BOSTON ON GOOD TERMS.

On the 2d of November, the last performance at Boston, for the benefit of Mdlle. Rachel.

VIRGINIE,
Tragedy in five acts, by Latour de Saint-Ybar.
And, by general request,
The French National Hymn,
LA MARSEILLAISE.

Receipts: 18,831 francs.

Virginie had a better success than anything we have played up to this time. The audience is positively enthusiastic. It applauds furiously, madly, not only Rachel, but all the artists in the leading parts: Chéry, aîné (*Fabius*), Raphaël Félix (*Appius*), and, finally, Randoux (*Virginius*), called for again, with Rachel, after the first act. At the close of the piece, they call everybody before the curtain, precisely as they do on the Boulevards.

As for that, there is really a Boulevard audience this evening—an audience warm, ardent, delighted to applaud. All the French in Boston are met at the theatre; almost all workmen. One positively imagines himself in Paris. Besides, the MARSEILLAISE produces, this evening, an effect unknown till now. It is a colossal success. This performance, receipts apart, is certainly Rachel's finest triumph. In order to have a nearer view of the great tragédienne, all the students of Cambridge University asked permission to take part in *Virginie.*

It was very curious, I assure you, to see all these young men, of the best American families, serving as supernumeraries in a French tragedy. What was also very amusing, was the earnestness with which they threw off their Roman dresses, to applaud in the wings this famous MARSEILLAISE.

As Rachel scarcely waited for the entr'acte, they all came down from their dressing-rooms, half-undressed. Some had their pantaloons and boots on, but had not yet quitted their tunics; others had black coats, and flesh-colored tights, etc., etc. In fact, it was truly grotesque to see the wings crowded with these burlesques without head or tail!

Going rather late to Bourguignon's, the man of squirrels, you know, we found all the Frenchmen who boarded with him engaged in emptying a respectable number of bottles of wine to the health of Rachel and the French Company. After which one of them struck up the MARSEILLAISE.

The police, finding probably that the song was being somewhat abused, came, very politely, to be sure, to request the gentlemen to conclude their musical exercise. "It was very late," said the policemen, "and the slumbers of the neighborhood were disturbed." No one had anything to say to that, and everybody went to bed; it was the best thing they could do.

The next day, at half-past five in the afternoon, *the French Company* take the cars again and quit this excellent town. At nine o'clock we take the steamer Vanderbilt and start for New York. Truly splendid affairs are these steamboats—immense. In this one there are, I think, 1,200 beds, an altogether unheard-of

10*

luxury. Each of these boats is worth at least a million.

Unfortunately we had on board a very lame supper. I had all the trouble in the world to eat one mouthful.

I addressed myself to a black servant, and asked him for some bread (in English, however). The negro brings me a fried egg. I demand a beef-steak. He serves me with a sausage.

I beseech him at last to grant me a glass of water, and the good negro brought me—what? —a fried fish.

This event by no means hinders the *Vanderbilt* from arriving next day, at a quarter past seven, at the port of New York.

Mademoiselle Rachel returns to her domicile in Clinton Place. Mademoiselle Sarah regains her abode in Broome street, and MM. Félix, as well as Mademoiselles Lia and Dinah, fugitives from Clinton Place, go down to the Hotel de l'Europe, where the rest of the company are already installed with bag and baggage.

Fifth Part.

RETURN TO NEW YORK.

CHAPTER I.

JULES JANIN IN THE UNITED STATES.

We innocently thought to find New York as we left it. Hardly have we landed, ere we remark a strange agitation in the city. Yes, groups are gathered in the streets, they converse with extraordinary animation. Every one wears an unnatural expression. They crack jokes. They talk as they walk along!

Dollar seems quite forgotten. Hardly, oh! wonderful! is the mastication of the morsel of traditional tobacco—that inseparable friend of every good Yankee—remembered; New York is evidently not is its ordinary mood. What has come to pass?

Has Kossuth made a new triumphal entry

into the first city of the Union? That is not to be imagined.

Have the elections gone wrong? It would not seem so. The banners they carry around, the guns which they madly fire under the very noses of the passers-by, the worn-out straw beds that they burn witlessly under the windows of the happy candidates—all prove that there is nothing to complain of on that score.

Is the British ensign floating on the public monuments, in the place of the American colors? No, the star-spangled banner is still there.

Are they afraid that the little earthquake on *Staten Island* is the prelude of some tremendous upheaving?

Fudge! they are by no means the sort of people to bother about such a trifle. "We'll take the consequences" is their motto.

And, apropos of consequences, a new railroad bridge has just tumbled down spilling all the cars into the river and piling them one upon another; may it not be this horrible catastrophe which gives them all such long faces? In all seven hundred people wounded, only twenty-five killed! Come, come, that is not sufficient to disturb the good-humor of such a philosophi cal people.

But really, what is this all about? There is—there is a number of the *Journal des Debats,* which an English steamer has just brought over from France, and this number contains an article by Jules Janin on Rachel and tragedy in the United States—and it is this article and nothing else, that stirs up this high excitement in the New Yorkish population.

Ah! if Janin had only been there! "These shop-keepers, fathers and sons of shop-keepers," as he contemptuously calls them, are literally ferocious about him.

Here is the revolutionary article—read and tremble!

"MADEMOISELLE RACHEL AND TRAGEDY IN THE UNITED STATES.

"At present the dramatic art is in trouble about Mademoiselle Rachel. For, after all, she is its queen, and if it should be so unfortunate as to lose her, she could never be replaced. She is our child, she was born under our wing, she has thrived under our nurturing. With her all-powerful breath she reanimated tragedy even in the coffin: 'Arise and walk!' and tragedy obeyed; and Corneille and Racine, whom we had thought dead, were rejuvenated by the accents of that irresistible voice. So the birth of this child, let us remember, was one of the high holidays of Poetry.

'The court of Apollo arose to honor her.'

This is why grateful spirits—that is to say, those who have prescience—inquire, not without anxiety, what has become of Mademoiselle Rachel, where is she at this hour, and to what land has she transferred—imprudent one—the graces, the sorrows, the loves, the bearing, and the passion of the old French world? To these questions there is as yet no answer; there are only murmurs, threats, nothing clear—and the anxiety redoubles, and Tragedy, despairing, calls back her Rachel.

"And we, too, in the midst of this general uneasiness, are possessed with a desire to know what, truly, at this day, is the strange nation to which Mademoiselle Rachel has carried her gods and her heroes; and when we ask the best instructed, this is the answer we get: 'The social state of the Americans is eminently democratic; it has had this character since the birth of the Colonies; it is still more so in our time.'

"These are the words of a master-historian, and that one phrase, 'essentially democratic,' was and must be, a threat for Mademoiselle Rachel. In fact, she belongs, by the art she cultivates, by the chefs-d'œuvre she represents, to all that republicanism, to all that monarchy presents, of elegance, of politeness, of cultivation, of aristocracy and refinement. Athens is a court; the Rome of Augustus is a court; Louis XIV. is a sun who gives light to the stars; the great poets, Euripides and Sophocles, Corneille and Racine, address themselves to choice spirits, to select souls, to elegant passions, to grandeur, to the all-powerful, to majesty. It is in a world apart, and very hard to please, that these great dramas are acted; they speak to the souls of a select few, much more than to the passions of the common crowd. They are drawn toward the idea, the sentiment, the ideal, and not to noise, tumult, and brutal sensations. If the herd loves loud cries, changes of view, and surprises, the court prefers correct emotions, clear and well explained events, fine language, the elegant murmur. It subjects everything to its whims, to its tastes, to its sense of propriety—everything, even its passions. Inasmuch as it is composed of a few cultivated men, subject to the same sceptre, and united under the same laws of etiquette and taste, it happens that the poets of this world unwittingly obey this sovereign will, that they neglect nothing which can please this circle of fine spirits; that they attach as much importance to their style as to their ideas; that they are concerned for the most trifling details; that, to a just degree, they seek above all things for whatever is noble and great; and that, in fine, only those who have early had the advantage of a literary education, and who have long learned in the school of the old masters, venture upon the difficult exercises of literature. 'It is no common praise,' said Horace, 'that one is capable of pleasing the men who govern us.' And Virgil, too, said,

'If we sing of forests, let the forests be worthy of consuls.'

"Thus the great art, the art *par excellence* of kings, and queens, and consuls, which Mademoiselle Rachel represents, is essentially the art of great princes, of famous ministers, the art of heroes and brilliant youths; it allies itself with the great arts of long ago, with the Athenian aristocracy, the Roman aristocracy, with the most polished nations, with the most instructed cities—with delicates tongues which regard the slightest innovation as a crime, and treat the least new word as an abominable barbarism.

"This is why, contrary to the first laws of democracy, wherein the majority is sovereign, in poetry, and in the art of which we speak, it is the minority which makes the law, it is the smaller number, the very small number, of people of taste, which dictates, which says which are the the chefs-d'œuvre. In a democracy, on the contrary, not only is it the majority which makes the law, which makes manners, but it also makes a language for its own use, at liberty to scratch out next morning what it laid down the day before. It despises, inexpressibly, the learned languages, which it calls the dead languages—as if the *Iliad* could die, as if the *Cid* could die. By as much as the elegant nations, of whom we have just spoken, hold themselves apart from the other nations, as if they feared to hurt by foreign contact the very heart of their poetry and the purity of their fine language, by even so much do these turbulent democracies make a point of spreading themselves abroad, and of reducing the language they speak to its simplest expression, in order that all may understand them and barter with them. In old Paris alone, consider how many different languages. The language of the *Place Royale* was not the language spoken at Versailles; the circle of the Duchess de Chaulnes had its own language; the saloon of Madame de Lafayette also. At that time there was the language of the street and that of the saloon, the language of savans and the vulgar language. The rich and the poor, the Parisian and the provincial, the captain and the magistrate, the priests and the literati, the nobleman and the citizen, spake not the same language; yet from these diverse tongues, skillfully melted and blended by genius, came the French of the classics; from this résumé of so many different languages, this tower of Babel of ivory and gold, came Pascal, came Molière, Corneille also, and Racine. On the contrary, the more a democracy is sovereign, the more it wishes to be heard and understood, here, there, and everywhere. It wishes, in fact, to 'speak as everybody speaks'—that is fair enough; but it also desires to write as it speaks, and that is why it is a fault, perhaps a crime, to offer to its unintelligence, to its scorn, works written two centuries and a half ago, in temples now overthrown and for dethroned monarchies, with such art, such harmony, such taste, that periods the most polished, the most charming, have produced nothing more exquisite, more rare, or more perfect.

"Truly, in order to understand and love these beautiful things as our fathers loved them, one should have been born in a sort of kindly sloth, far from labor and the daily ambitions of the vulgar. One should be a man of leisure to love Racine; he should come of ancestors who have filled a certain rôle in story, and in the emotions of the Past, if he would transport himself with delight, with pride, back to the fêtes, the sorrows, the struggles of ancient history.

"An ancient people willingly looks back upon its past, because it is sure to be at home in the battles, the conquests, and the generous struggles of its youth; but a people of yesterday finds nothing of interest in a period in which its name was unknown. Try and interest Americans in the origin of Rome, and the afflictions of the old Horatius; make their tradesmen, the sons of navigation and of commerce, understand the noble thoughts expressed in this line:

"'Si vous n'êtes Romains, soyez dignes de l'être.'

"Immediately, the American stares at you, astonished; anxiously he inquires what the young Horatius says; he knows not that the Roman work was to accomplish, generously, noble things; to suffer, bravely, great misfortunes.

"No American can understand the state of a new-born community, where every man is a hero; on the contrary, this heroism of the three Horatii and the three Curiatii disturbs the implacable equality of the American Democracy; the latter is willing that the people may be great, but on condition that every man composing the people shall be of the same height; so that, in a democratic nation, there can be no heroism and no heroes. Tarquin, walking in a garden of New York, would not find a single poppy-head to strike down; all the poppies there are equally tall! It would be vain for a poet to seek for a hero in this restless and turbulent nation, which would neither accept Ajax, nor Hector, nor the sage Ulysses, and which would give three groans for Agamemnon, the king of kings!

"O, hapless poet, how I should pity you, you who live among legends, traditions, recollections, if you should essay to content yourself with this multitude, where all the men have the same talent, the same appearance, and, as for that, the same name.

"Thus, Aristocracy was one of the necessary

conditions of ancient poetry; it was, above all, one of the conditions of the old dramatic art; a single family—only one—suffices for the labors of three Greek masters.

> "'La colère d'Achille, avec art ménagée,
> Remplit abondamment une *Iliade* entière.'

"Democracy, on the other hand, spares nothing. It uses, it abuses, it bellows, it flies into a rage; it troubles itself but little about probabilities, and less about truth. It piles Ossa upon Pelion, and Pelion upon Ossa; neither manners, nor history, nor the Past, nor the Future, embarrass the poets of Democracy; without rule or rhythm, they traverse the absurd; after all, what matters it to them whether they write well or ill. Their play once out of the theatre, they are very sure no one will read it.

For such a people, the name of their heroes is Legion. They acknowledge no royalties; they despise sceptres; they trample crowns under their feet; and nothing annoys them more than the importance and the majesty of certain great men in the destinies of the world, and in the admiration of poesy. So that when Mdlle. Rachel brings to these tradesmen, sons and fathers of tradesmen, a sort of elegy in five acts, called "Cinna," in which the Emperor Augustus dares to say, in the presence of an American audience—

"'Cet empire absolu sur la terre et sur l'onde,
Ce pouvoir souverain, que j'ai sur tout le monde,'

she insults the assumptions of the people. The New World knows nothing of the Roman dominion; it does not wish to know anything of it, and if you are obstinate enough to insist on discoursing of greatness not its own; to tell it of a world of which it is ignorant—a world which knew nothing beyond Rome—you wound it in its pride, in its ambition, and all the passions born of Democracy. The voice which, from the middle of the astonished pit, interrupted Mdlle. Rachel when playing Emilie, and called for the 'Marseillaise,' (sic,) was the genuine voice of a Democrat, and called for the only tragedy and the only drama which Democracy can love and comprehend—the tumultuous drama of the mob yelling at the cross-roads—the tragedy of a people trampling under foot all the greatness of the times. A Democrat would give, gladly, and as if he were making a good bargain, every classic part of Mdlle. Rachel—the grace, the elegance, the chaste love, the honorable inspiration of great men, the courage and the chastity of illustrious princesses—for that horrible song of exile, of murder, and the scaffold—

"'Qu'un sang impur abreuve nos sillons!'

"To this impious request—one which she only too much deserved—she did not reply with the horror which it ought to have excited in her. It is true she refused to chant the 'Marseillaise,' saying that she no longer had the necessary voice. She ought to have replied as follows: 'What! I came here, my brains filled with master-pieces, my hands laden with palms and crowns! I bring you the miracles of three centuries, Augustus, Pericles, and Louis XIV., and you demand la Marseillaise! I bring you Corneille and Racine, and you call for Sauterre and Danton! Leave me! You are unworthy of such great fortune, and you are incapable of understanding so much sacred sorrow, so much brilliant majesty!'

"Thus should she have spoken, and at once left the country. She did not know—our imprudent Rachel—into what gulf she was going to fall! She did not know what a thing it is to amuse, night after night, tradesmen insensible to the charms of accent, voice, gesture; insensible to learned speech, to the soul and spirit of ancient genius. She supposed, remembering her former wanderings, that she could do without princesses to defend her, and kings to applaud her; she did not reckon among her European successes the favor of the Queen of England, the interest of the King of Prussia, the kindness of the Court of St. Petersburg, the innate and habitual elegance of courtiers, of warriors, of ladies of honor, of those grand lords who call Tragedy their queen, who call Corneille their father, and who made Racine their god! She did not see that the master-pieces she carried with her were, to these privileged minds, the glorious echoes of the age of Monarchies—the *Cid*, which caused Richelieu to spend sleepless nights; *Iphigenia*, that won a smile from Mme. de Montespan; *Cinna*, which drew tears from the Prince de Conde!

"Le grand Condé pleurant aux vers du grand Corneille!

"Poor child! poor Rachel! she took all to herself in her progress through intelligent Europe; for her all those bravos, for her all those crowns; and, nevertheless, the attentive companions of her pilgrimage: Hermione, Emilie, Horace, Andromaque, Pauline and Polyeucte, Athalie and the little king, Joas—these beauties, these virgins, these heroes, this divine language, this poetry, made expressly for the ears of gods, for the hearts of lovers, for the minds of sages, for these souls apart, in the ordering and government of the human race—these opened all the doors to Rachel; they were of her company, she was in their confidence. They lived together; they spoke the divine language which is spoken in the high places of the world, between earth and sky, on the border of the clear fountain, where the Muses and Graces still reign above the storms. And, therefore, all the doors of all the monarchies open before Mademoiselle Rachel; therefore these eager advances, therefore this partiality.

"'Welcome to Elsinore,' said a courtier

of Hamlet of Denmark to the poor comedians.

" 'The court was her country; for from the court she no longer has either hearth or homestead,' said Madame de Sevigné of an exiled princess. We may say of Mademoiselle Rachel:

"She is lost, away from the thrones and courts. In that feverish American democracy, it is she that is the barbarian, because she is not understood, because she has neither home nor fireside there; she is a vagabond, errant comédienne, she tells of sorrows in which her audiences do not believe. Why exhibit to Americans, Monime prostrate at the knees of Mithridates, expiring? Mithridates is no worse off than Uncle Tom! For they have gone no further than Uncle Tom in tragedy! Uncle Tom is the American Agamemnon, the American Achilles! It is he that is hissed, admired, loved, abused; he is their hero, their buffoon, their martyr! The only American Parthenon is 'Uncle Tom's Cabin!' Uncle Tom is their Odyssey—their Iliad!

"It is worth remarking, that, with a little foresight, Mademoiselle Rachel might easily have convinced herself that she was destined to pass through a thousand deaths, in her talent, in her influence, in her pride. Had she looked into any American book before leaving, she would have better understood the American multitude, subdued, or rather gulled, by the great Barnum at his pleasure. For, though they resist Iphigenia, though they go to sleep before the furies of Orestes, though they call Corneille stupid; yet, at the beck of Barnum, they rush to see a stuffed mermaid, or, seated in her filth and her drivel, an old, black, idiot mummy, whose hideous teats suckled the great Washington! And these heroes of equality, though they believed the old woman to have been really the nurse of their great man, their savior, not one of them thought of snatching the poor old thing from the hands of the showman. Say to Frenchmen, on the contrary, 'Here is the mother of Voltaire,' and they will fall on their two knees before her.

"So I say, that Mademoiselle Rachel, with a very slight effort—had she merely looked over a late work by Madame Marie Fontenay, entitled 'L'Autre Monde,'—would have found in it details upon the other world, which would have certainly made her stay in this one.

" Surely, we do not attach more credit than they deserve to the words of Madame Marie Fontenay; but then she is a woman; she is of that ripe age when one sees well whatever one sees at all; she returns from this old New World, relating a thousand stories which are not in praise of the fine arts, and the fine passions of New York. For example, she will tell you what *flirtation* is, that is to say, what love is in the United States. 'Tis a certain license, permitted to the young marriageable girl, of going and coming, without danger to her reputation, and without danger to her heart. She flirts; she gads; she is like a lovely flower, which every one inhales, which no one must touch. More than all things she wishes for a husband, and she asks not what he is, but how much is he worth. Alas, how little does this flirtation resemble the love of Hermione; alas! how could this errant damsel, in search of a husband, who, first of all, must be rich, be entertained by hearing a Greek princess say to Cléone:

"'Non Cléone, il n'est point ennemi de lui-même ;
Il veut tout ce qu'il fait ; et s'il m'epouse, il m'aime.'

"Certainly, it is a pretty thing, this *flirtation;* but the passion, the eloquence, and the proud content of a loving heart.

—"'Eh bien ! chère Cléone,
Conçois-tu les transports de l'hereuse Hermione ?
Sais-tu quel est Pyrrhus ? T'es-tu fait raconter
Le nombre des exploits.... Mais qui les peut compter ?
Intrépide et partout suivi de la victoire,
Charmant, fidèle, enfin rien ne manque à sa gloire !'

"The beautiful accents, the majestic words! In those times, they did not flirt, they loved. The princess was guarded; she obeyed the strictest laws of obedience and duty; she did not go out to sup, in full flirtation, with gentlemen, at 'one of the luxurious restaurants in which New York abounds.' Moreover, when a princess by chance got into an omnibus (fortunately, there were no omnibuses for French princesses), she did not seat herself on the knees of the nearest man. But now that is done in New York, flirtation apart. And how delightfully such a jaunt in an omnibus, on some fellow's knees, fits her to hear and appreciate this fine discourse of the loving Orestes!

"'Ah! Madame! est-il vrai qu'une fois
Oreste en vous cherchant obéisse a vos lois?
Ne m'a-t-on pas flatté d'une fausse espérance?
Avez-vous en effet souhaité ma présence?'

"Let us add here, that American women hold in profound scorn this amiable and charming condition; to be an honored woman—loved, admired, but loved and admired from a distance: to have all the graces, all the elegancies, all the adornments of a woman—diamonds, and all manner of jewels, fine clothes, flattering attachments. No, they must be men—that is at once their glory and their ambition. Happiness, cheerfulness of heart, they renounce for muslin, velvet, embroidered petticoats, and even love affairs, which make a little noise, when poets sing them. 'There is one thing as dead as the tomb,' says our voyageuse to America, 'and that is the love of an American woman.' Ah! then, if they are so very discreet, why relate to them all those charming and famous love passages, which brought tears into the sweetest eyes at the courts of Augustus and Louis XIV.?

"An American woman hates the distaff; she would be ashamed to say, as the adopted child of Montaigne, Mademoiselle de Gournay, said to a handsome officer who defied her—'I wager my distaff against your sword!' In revenge, they sport manly attire; they are Bloomerists; apparelled in blouses, disguised in pantaloons, they go about preaching Woman's Rights. Oh! oh! picture to yourself a club of women in the midst of Paris, in the evenings when the *Marseillaise* was sung; when old art gave place to all the riot of the streets; and then put, if you choose, some bloused Bloomerist, or the president of the Women's Club, in the front boxes, while Iphigenia, at her father's feet, imploring him with the deep and tender gaze of a fond maiden of sixteen summers, who clings to life yet wishes to obey, cries to him, choking down her tears—

"'——— Mon père,
Cessez de vous troubler; vous n'êtes point trahi:
Quand vous commanderez, vous serez obéi.
Ma vie est votre bien: vous voulez le reprendre;
Vos ordres sans détour pouvaient se faire entendre.
D'un œil aussi content, d'un cœur aussi soumis
Que j'acceptai l'époux que vous m'aviez promis,
Je saurai, s'il le faut, victime obéissante,
Tendre au fer de Calchas une tête innocente,
Et, respectant le coup par vous-même ordonné,
Vous rendre tout le sang que vous m'avez donné.'

"Declaim these beautiful sentiments in the presence of Bloomerists, and they will claim liberty to speak in full theatre for a personal explanation. They will say this Iphigenia is a fool, that she carries her filial obedience too far. A father, a husband, a man, marriage, a tragedy in verse—what do you think of them? And what will the famous Editor of the NEW YORK TRIBUNE say? In effect, that paternal authority, these sweet fancies, these cherished existences, have no great run in a country where the boy goes free at twelve, and meeting his brother or his sister, asks by-the-byishly, 'How is the old man?' The old man is his father, and the old woman is his mother. Then shout in his ears, which are steeled on the side of his heart, what Andromache says to Pyrrhus:

"'Je passais jusqu'aux lieux où l'on garde mon fils;
Puisqu'une fois le jour vous souffrez que je voie
Le seul bien qui me reste et d'Hector et de Troie,
J'allais, seigneur, pleurer un moment avec lui;
Je ne l'ai point encore embrassé d'aujourd'hui!'

"If the son of Hector were in New York, he would already know the four rules of arithmetic, and would earn every day his half-dollar and pay board to his mother, Andromache. You remember the fine dispute between Agamemnon and the terrible Achilles—that grand scene of defiance between two formidable warriors—the young man carried away by love, beyond all bounds—while the father, the king, meets this fury with self-command and majesty. What would you do with that admirable scene, a marvel of our old dramatic art, in a country where everybody carries a ten-shot revolver in his left pocket, a dirk in his right pocket, and takes the law into his own hands in the streets, or in full Senate; or even if, by chance, a regular duel is arranged, the two men take their guns and beat about for each other in an open field, as we hunt a boar or wolf.

ACHILLE

" 'Rendez grâce au seul nœud qui retient ma colère,
D'Iphigénie encor je respecte le père;
Peut-être sans ce nom, le chef de tant de rois
M'aurait osé braver pour la dernière fois.'

What sort of way is that? Why the devil don't he draw a six-barrel at once?

"I look also in this instruction book of Mme. Fontenay, which might have served Mdlle.

Rachel, for what the Americans like best after an abolition harangue or a Bloomer speech—it certainly is not the theatre, and it is not music, in spite of Jenny Lind, Giulia Grisi, Mario, or the unfortunate Madame Sontag, who has just died: what they prefer to anything else, are tame bears, mountebanks, boxers, and the *tours de force* of tight-rope dancers, which they are very careful to call *acrobats* or *funambulists;* it is strange that although new people hate Greek and Latin, they voluntarily apply little bits of it here and there to everything low and ludicrous. For people who enjoy these things, imagine their astonishment when we gave them *Athalie* or *Polyeucte*, and Mdlle. Rachel in the wonderful character of Pauline:

"*'Je vois, je sais, je crois, je suis désabusée!'*

"Ah! what beautiful fêtes those were for us in the fine old days of yore. Such grand soirées! *Polyeucte! Athalie!* Oh! masterpieces which will live for ever in all honest hearts, in all intelligent souls! In those days, throughout Paris, the noblest houses, old Christian families, forgetting their antipathy and prejudices against the stage, led to this enchanted palace their youngest children, their young girls, impelled by a sort of irresstiible impulse, the splendor and grace of these old houses—offsprings of royalty, of established faith; and the wisest fathers, the most prudent mothers, said to their bewildered children: Look, listen, weep as you please, there is no harm in it, there is nothing to fear, on the contrary, everything is beautiful and blessed in these fêtes of Saint Cyr and Port Royal! Children, listen to *Athalie*, it belongs to Madame de Maintenon as much as to Racine; listen also to *Polyeucte*. M. Arnauld and Mother Angelica Arnauld read *Polyeucte!* And the young ones, beautiful and adorned with their grace and their youth. Mothers in their finest attire, fathers and grandfathers in full dress, took part in these fêtes of their youth. There was nothing finer, you will recollect, Rachel, in the Théâtre Français, then these august solemnities of poetry and high dramatic art; we had truly, under our very eyes, Spring itself, and everybody kept silent to let these children applaud; their beautiful, dazzled eyes, their little trembling hands, serious lips, and thoughtful brows, threw even additional splendor over the exquisite verses. What grand soirées! alas! and what a brilliant crowd! What glory and good fortune for the French comedians who were called upon to celebrate great master-pieces before these gay assemblages of French aristocracy, unequalled by any under the sun—the aristocracy of name, of genius, of intelligence, of studious and classic beauties, for which you would in vain search elsewhere. You might find fragments of it, mere recollections and echoes; but united and entire in its present, its past, and its future, you will find it only on such choice days as I have spoken of, in the presence of some *chef-d œuvre* of Christian art.

"Please God, Mademoiselle Rachel may not try to play *Athalie* or *Polyeucte* in America, with Bloomers in the first circle and negresses and negroes up above, staring at the phantom —she would be compelled in these cruel, painful occasions to make mortifying comparisons!

"Do you know, for instance, in what way Americans applaud the finest things and greatest artists. *They whistle.* With the Americans, to whistle, to yell, is to applaud.

"It is hard to believe the pass to which American impertinence often reaches (it is still Madame Fontenay who speaks, and we quote her, word for word). At railroad stations, as in hotel saloons, it is not unusual to see them, with dirty shoes, and hat on head, brutally stretched on the seats or sofas. The boats on the Northern lakes, which are luxuriously furnished, have a special regulation which imposes a fine on every passenger who goes to bed with his boots on.

"And this article of the same regulation relating to meals, requires gentlemen to take seats at table after the ladies. But the Americans do not take this rule seriously, and are at their ease there as they are everywhere else.

"Leaving out of the question the articles of claret, sherry, and whisky, let us also forget that these messieurs love to stick their feet against the wall, and are not at their ease unless their heads are on the floor and their feet in the air.

"The Americans have another way which

must much disturb Mademoiselle Rachel when on the stage, unless they have sacrificed their tastes and passions at her shrine. For it is the custom of every American to have continually in his hand a pen or jack knife, and to whittle famously at the arm of his chair; this is his distinction, his occupation, and his amusement, for it kills both time and tragedy. It would seem, nevertheless, as though the progress of the play might be disturbed by these makers of shavings, and that the tragédienne, accustomed to profound silence, to the feverish attention of every eye, of every soul hanging upon her lips, must be strangely stupefied and troubled on hearing these strokes and cuttings of knives, fit at the very best to accompany a rope-dancer or a boxer in the ring.

"Now I do not mean to say that the American democracy is to be blamed for remaining faithful to its customs, to its tastes, and admirations, and that it ought at once to renounce cigars and whisky, Uncle Tom and whittling, dirty boots and Bloomerism, simply because Mademoiselle Rachel sought to initiate it into the great works of another period. I am certainly not so imprudent as to desire thus suddenly, apropos of an actress on her travels, to remould and correct a whole people. But at least through respect for our chefs-d'œuvre, through pity for the greatest artist of our time, let us expose them no longer to the disdains of a democracy.

"Perhaps, and I am inclined to hope so, Mdlle. Rachel has already seen enough to understand that she does not speak the language of the country; that the people there do not know a single word of the stories she has to tell; and that the charming and terrible mysteries of the antique muse are altogether out of place there. She must already have felt, and every day she will feel it more keenly, that it is she who is the barbarian, because she is not understood; she will soon, I trust, leave the country to the bears, the street-preachers, the tumblers, the Barnums, and the usual amusements of the American people. She has shown herself, she has gained her cause, and can well afford to pay the expenses. And then her return will be so triumphant, especially if she return before her promise! We shall be so glad to see her again, especially if we are to console her for deceptions and disappointments over there!

"The more difficulties she has to encounter in that matter-of-fact country, the more success she will meet with in one of refinement, where it is considered a triumph even to speak so correctly the only language made for a polite people. So her disgrace, even—if disgrace it is—will increase the popularity of Mdlle. Rachel with us. We love her, we want her; it has been always with regret that we have permitted her to go to foreign countries, from which she has always returned a little weakened and a little deteriorated.

"This lesson, happily, will be her last; and we are all willing to think that we have not paid too dear for it. Shall we not be enchanted to see our Rachel snatched from that noise and tumult, half applause, half hisses (*sic*), which must disgust her to the very bottom of her soul!

"It has been happily said, that if the triangles made a god, they would give him three sides; if the Americans ever made a *tragédienne*, I don't know how they will do it; but it will not be according to the image of the Venus of Milo, the tragedies of Corneille, or Mdlle. Rachel.

"Let her return to us; she will be welcomed once again; the sooner the greater the rejoicing.

"'So, Madame, it is only necessary to go to Spain, to lose the desire of building castles there,' said Madame la Marquise de Villars to Madame de Maintenon.

"JULES JANIN."

Certainly, when he says that the Americans are "a stirring, excitable people, who would have neither Ajax nor Hector, nor the wise Ulysses, and who would treat even Agamemnon, king of kings, to three groans," Janin was not altogether wrong; he is even far from being so when he adds: "They repulse Iphigenia, go to sleep over the furies of Orestes; and they call Corneille a dotard; but if Barnum chooses, they rush to behold a stuffed mermaid, or to see, slobbering in filth, an old black, idiotic mummy, whose hideous nipple has suckled the great Washington, because Barnum tells them to do so." Doubtless, this is all true.

"The son of Hector, in New York, would understand already the four rules, would earn his half-dollar a day, and would pay his board to his mother Andromache." Evidently, what is preferred in America, "is not the theatre, is not music, in spite of Jenny Lind, Giulia Grisi, Mario, and the unfortunate Madame Sontag, who has just died;— but tame bears, mountebanks, boxing, and the *tours de force* of tight-rope dancers."

But who likes all this? The masses—the masses, who are unintelligent and gross in the United States, as they are everywhere else.

And these "Barnumries"! does any one believe that the Press waits to be urged, to do such exhibitions severe and prompt justice? No! no more than it hesitated to write upon Rachel and French tragedy perfectly correct and impartial criticisms. And this is why the Press, furious at being so misunderstood, hurls against Parisian critics such thunder-bolt articles.

There is still one thing to remark; and that is, that the most bitter New York journalist is a Frenchman, one of the editors of the *Courrier des Etats-Unis!*

Finally, everybody is angry with Janin. French people will not forgive him for having treated Rouget de L'Isle and his Marseillaise so cavalierly in his article; the Americans are outraged at being accused by him of imploring for this same Marseillaise, when they had never dreamed of it; and much more for having demanded it during the play of *Cinna*, in which Rachel never performed in the United States. And Rachel, Rachel herself is not better pleased than the others! It was in vain that Janin wrote: "She is our child, born under our wing! She has made herself great in our language;" *his child* is none the less provoked, although *born under his wing*, to hear him make use of this very *language, in which she has made herself great*, to cry aloud to the whole world that her campaign in America is, after all, only an immense defeat.

CHAPTER II.

IN WHICH WE SCARCELY KNOW TO WHAT THEATRE TO DEVOTE OURSELVES.

During, and in spite of, the excitement produced by the article just mentioned, the performances of Mademoiselle Rachel continued to take place no longer at the Metropolitan, but at the Academy of Music. It is an immense house, but badly arranged. It is impossible to see plainly from all sides; there are no decorations and no stage-properties; it is old and faded; it puts suicide in one's head to go in there! Precisely like the *Odéon* ten years ago! Add to this that this poor theatre is two miles from the centre of the city, and that the New Yorkers have realized in this case the famous jest that has been made so often at the expense of this same *Odéon*—they take the railroad to go there. A mule railroad, it is true; but still a railroad.

The performances of Mademoiselle Rachel alternate with those of Madame A. de Lagrange, of the Opera (Paris).

On the 5th of November, Madame de Lagrange plays *Fidès*, in the first representation of the

PROPHETE,

very poorly gotten up as to scenery, costumes, and mise-en-scène generally; and the next evening Mademoiselle Rachel recommences her performances in New York, by the everlasting

ADRIENNE LECOUVREUR,

which, notwithstanding its reputation, made in all 8,526 francs. Yes, 8,526 francs only, in this immense house; it was horrible to contemplate! This representation was coldly received: applause here and there, but never a laugh!

The night but one after the first performance in America of

LADY TARTUFFE,

the receipts are even less satisfactory than those of night before last: 8,515 francs. That is bad. This theatre is decidedly a failure. Mademoiselle Rachel wishes to leave it at any risk. Raphaël, who, for his part, asks nothing better than to rid himself immediately of this gigantic shop, doesn't say two words on the subject, but goes at once in quest of another house. He finds one nearly opposite the Metropolitan, in Broadway, a very pretty little saloon, *ma foi!* as gay-looking as the Academy was lugubrious, and rejoicing in the lively name of Niblo's Garden. (The garden of *Niblo!*)

On the 12th, at this new theatre, the receipts increased to 14,007 francs with

ANGELO.

The next night, 12,941 francs, made with

LE CHAPEAU D'UN HORLOGER, AND VIRGINIE.

For *Angelo*, we found nearly everything necessary for stage-properties and scenery; but for *Virginie* it was otherwise—impossible to procure anything. Instead of a Roman interior, we have a little Louis XVth chamber. As to tragic accessories, they are utterly wanting. Not the smallest Lar! which distresses Mademoiselle Rachel, who doesn't want to play without her Lars! That will be understood.

The last act of this *Virginie* is truly comic. The Forum is replaced by a view of our Parisian boulevards. At the back, on the left, is a large house, with this sign in large letters—RESTAURANT. Gas-burners and Rambutian monuments in every direction. To complete the picturesqueness of the scene, there is a flowered carpet in the middle of the street.

As to the supernumeraries of this tragedy, nothing ever equalled them.

These supernumeraries are costumed by the theatre, which, accustomed only to getting up fairies, has no kind of toga or Roman tunic; so that the supernumeraries, the plebeians, are all villainously dressed à la jockey, in the *middle age* style of the Spaniards. As to the one hundred lictors of *Appius*, they are represented by twenty impossible men, disguised as devils—long yellowish gowns, red petticoats, sky-blue tights; and, to complete that, an "imperial" à l'Americaine, on their chin, a large tin spade in their hands, and, on their feet, old, worn-out boots. The Americans themselves could not maintain their dignity before this grotesque company.

On the 15th, the first representation of

MADEMOISELLE DE BELLE-ISLE.

CAST.

Richelieu, - - - - -	MM.	Latouche.
D'Aubigny, - - - - -	"	Randoux.
Le Marquis, - - - - -	Mlles.	Sarah.
Mlle. de Belle-Isle, - - - -	"	RACHEL.

This piece produced a great effect, and the receipts amounted to 15,760 francs! What a fortunate thing for us to have left the Academy of Music!

Mademoiselle Rachel had not, however, bid an eternal adieu to that lugubrious house. She performed there again, on the 16th, for the benefit of Madame de Lagrange.

They gave the first act of

I PURITANI.

Then the Second Act of

ATHALIE,

by RACHEL.

And finally the two last Acts of

I PURITANI.

This recalled to us that representation of *Tartuffe*, at the *Odéon*, in which they interpolated, between the second and third acts of Molière's chef-d'œuvre, I have forgotten what one act comedy, because Bocage would not appear till a certain hour.

This newly-discovered point of resemblance with that of the *Odéon* does not prevent this representation from being very fine.

Rachel was magnificent as *Athalie*, and Madame Lagrange wonderful in *Elvira*.

After the first act they showered on the *bénéficiare*, not only applause and bouquets, but tame doves. Since we are talking of doves, and since these birds, who have dragged for so long the car of Venus, that they must be slightly fatigued, enjoy, with cats, the privilege of being the most amorous of animals, we will take advantage of the suggestion to say a few words about a certain society which just now forms the charm of the New York populace. The Free Love League. That is its name. And the members of this tender association call themselves, naturally enough, "Free Lovers." New York is the established head-quarters. The meetings are held at the Tabernacle; price of admission, twenty-five cents. In this society, the great law of sympathy is the only one they feel bound to obey; there, all previous marriages are ignored. According to its code, every married "Free Lover" has a right to abandon his wife for another woman who pleases him more, and, on the other hand, every married woman can, in her turn, under the nose of her legitimate husband, respond to the advances of any "Free Lover," whoever he may be, with whom she sympathizes. We shall have much to say to you about this, but the name alone of the institution exempts us from the necessity of more ample details. Free love! that tells the whole story, and a great deal else beside.

CHAPTER III.

ADIEU TO NEW YORK.

The day after the benefit of Mme. Lagrange, there was given, at the last appearance of Rachel in New York,

PHEDRE,
by Rachel.
LE MOINEAU DE LESBIE,
by Rachel.
RACHEL A L'AMERIQUE,
An Ode, by
M. de Trobriand,

recited, of course, by Rachel.

This evening the receipts were 20,601 francs, and these 20,601 francs protest, by their frantic applause, against the article of the *Débats*. They have never been so enthusiastic before. This wakes them up. They have taken their time for it; but better late than never. Welcome to their enthusiasm.

Above all, during the recitation of the lines

of M. de Trobriand, their champion of the *Courrier*, they abandoned themselves to huzzas prolonged indefinitely, and to the most extraordinary stamping.

The ode is as follows:

"RACHEL TO AMERICA.

"Land of the Future, which a faith sublime
Fills with rich increase, Hail! though conquered time
Not yet for thee has harvested the Past,
Thy seed through far horizons now is cast,
And grander spaces open for thy hand:
Thy skies are blue, and green thy fruitful land,
Ages shall pass before thy youth shall see
Fulfilled the promise of thine infancy.

"How many nations, in their ripest days,
Knew not that halo of success which plays
Around thy cradle, young America!
Sprung, like the ancient Pallas, into day,
All armed; and even in thy natal hour
The world beheld thy lineage and thy power.

"Sleep, sleep in peace, in still funereal shade,
Ye heroes, once for battle's shock arrayed,
Who for your land and Freedom fought of old!
Not vainly then your hands her flag unrolled;
Your sons have followed you—your native shore
Sees risen on the banner that ye bore
More stars of peace upon its azure field,
Than e'er that hallowed war of yours could yield.

"Ye, victors, then returned to trench the soil,
And gave recruits to swell the ranks of Toil;

Peopled the wild, laid low the forest's gloom,
Sowed the rich soil, and made the waste to bloom,
And trampling strife and civil discord down,
Where reigned the desert, improvised the town!
Thus nobly toil, America! thy men;
Thy soldier thus becomes thy citizen.

"It was but yesterday; and now, behold!
Around her sovereign realm two oceans rolled:
Rich, great, and strong, with fearless heart and free,
She marches forward shouting 'Liberty!'

"O shade of Washington, look from thy rest!
Behold how thine illustrious work is blest—
Thy toiling people recognize with pride,
And be thy glorious spirit still their guide!
Keep them united in their hive, that they
May mark with miracles each passing day!

"When first the grandeurs which surround you gave
That growing charm which drew me o'er the wave,
They said to me; 'Seek not yon distant strand,
'Alien to thee the spirit of the land.
'Their life is work: they ask for hands alone,
'And not for genius: strange to them the tone
'Of grand Corneille, unknown his very name.
'Go not!' they counselled me: and so—I came.

"A trusting envoy, I have with me brought
My hopes, my oracles, my gods of thought;
The words of genius here my lips renew,
And silence those whose tongues would slander you.
Your answer here I read, and read with pride,
Too frank and honest for my heart to hide.
'Tis as I felt—all great things in the mind
Of a great people nobler greatness find.

"No future, from the memory of to-day,
Shall dim the picture which I bear away—
Whose charm will follow, where my steps depart,
To guide my efforts and to cheer my heart:
And this the glory henceforth I pursue—
Since you adopt me, to be worthy you."

It remains to be ascertained whether these last lines embody just at present the private opinions of the eminent tragédienne.

An American, Monsieur Taylor,* had translated into English verse M. de Trobriand's ode. This translation, I was told, was exceedingly remarkable. Which fact proves that what we were saying just now is perfectly true, and that in the United States, as everywhere else, only the masses lack refinement and intelligence!

* Bayard Taylor.

CHAPTER IV.

WHICH IS ALL ABOUT GAMBLING-HOUSES AND ROBBERS.

Before taking our eternal flight from the first city of the Union, let us glance, in passing, over the Broadway gambling-houses. Gambling-houses are one of the specialities of New York.

This kind of establishment can be found everywhere, in all parts of the city, in every street, at every corner. There is nothing astonishing in that; it is forbidden by law.

To make your way into these estimable saloons, you must be introduced by one who knows the ropes!

If anybody shows you this delusive kindness, so much the worse for you!

When this formality is complied with, the keeper, or one of the keepers of the house, a gentleman who does not give himself any airs, and who speaks to everybody, begs you, with enchanting affability, to be so good as to pass into the supper room, where a charming supper is served up! Do you like game? Here is game! Poultry? There is poultry! Roast meats? Side dishes? Dessert? There is everything! And what wine do you prefer? Bordeaux? Champagne? Both, perhaps! Very well! Steward fill this gentleman's glasses!

Now do you know how much they ask for this supper? Not even a thank you! It is not dear! Wait awhile!

This faro! this good old faro of the eighteenth century, which is still cultivated here in the next room! Do you call this nothing?

Do you think, then, that you have the courage to stay here and not throw down a few dollars on these cards, which are making faces at you on the green!

To be there and not play! Impossible! And to play at faro and not lose, still more impossible!

That is precisely why these gentlemen, well-got-up, sprinkled with jewels and enamelled with diamonds, offer you such good suppers gratis!

But these are nothing! There are other places, regular gambling-holes, they are; the dens of the Five Points! If you pass by these infamous places, real brigands' caves, step quick and do not stop to look over your shoulders!

Above all, never set your foot over the threshold of these lugubrious hovels; murders are done in there, throats are cut! The frequenters of these dens play cards with shabby coats, sleeves rolled up, a pipe in their mouths, a loaded revolver by their sides, and a well-sharpened knife under their hands!

To visit these charming places there must be five or six of you armed to the teeth; and you must, necessarily, be shown around by a policeman, who, for the sum of five dollars, does not refuse anybody this slight service! Without these precautions they would be perfectly sure of you! Ah! the society is charming.

Tell me, then, about these jolly thieves who amused themselves the other night in Thompson Street, by stealing two houses, of two stories apiece! That is odd, to say the least; is it not?

These two houses were wooden, as is too

much the custom in this country; the thieves tore them in pieces and carried away everything, to the last rail. They will put them together again somewhere else, and are, no doubt, a good deal vexed that they could not take the lots away at the same *time*!

The proprietor of these two houses was in the country. He must have been slightly astonished when he came home! Before closing this chapter, we will give you an item of news which has just come fresh from the United States:

All the Broadway gambling-houses are closed. The government decided to lose patience and rap these faro gentlemen over the knuckles a little. Everything was seized. As to the proprietors of these nocturnal establishments, they put them in prison for a little while, just to see! Let us pity them, but not let them out!

CHAPTER V.

IN WHICH IS TO BE SEEN A PLAY OF IMAGINATION.

However picturesque what you have just been reading may seem, it is at least a hundred leagues short of the odd fantasy which is now performing at the Bowery Theatre, and which is called on the bills with sublime assurance Bombardment of Sebastopol.

In this play of the imagination—

1st. The English alone take the Malakoff tower; there is not a Frenchman with them;

2nd. An American, the funny fellow of the piece, arrives in the Russian camp and offers his services to Gortschakoff, who accepts them gratefully. And he is very right in doing so, considering that in the next minute this same American defeats alone an entire battalion of English, which brings the whole house down;

3rd. And finally, there is nothing in this

étude historique, in the shape of a Frenchman, but an old Sergeant of Zouaves! At least they say he is an old Sergeant of Zouaves; he has the costume of a Neapolitan fisherman, surmounted by a Greek cap.

Apropos of theatres, we will mention a little fact, which will give an idea of what is understood by democracy on the other side of the water.

In the State of New York, in Pennsylvania, in Massachusetts, and in many other Northern States, where the Republican party is in power, slavery has been, and remains abolished. Well, it is precisely in those States that colored people are prohibited from entering a place of amusement. In the Slave States, the negroes have a reserved gallery in every theatre. What eternal contradictions! What the deuce can a man take seriously in this country?

At last, thank God, it is half-past five. It is the exact minute to go on board a steamboat, and make an end of it, at once, with this brave city of New York.

In twenty-five minutes we are on the other side of the river.

At six o'clock, we take the railroad, express train, and, exactly at ten, we reach the confines of the State of New York, and find ourselves on the banks of this famous river, the Delaware, which alone lies between us and Philadelphia.

We leave our wagons, go on board a steamboat again, and land, fifteen minutes afterwards, in the capital of Pennsylvania—the Quaker city, as it is called—one of the richest, handsomest, and most flourishing cities in the United States of America.

Sixth Part.

THE QUAKER CITY.

CHAPTER I.

KILLING TIME IN PHILADELPHIA.

ALTHOUGH the Indian summer is not yet over, it does not prevent us from having frightfully cold weather.

Winter is coming on with great strides.

In Canada, snow is falling already furiously, and sleighs are furrowing all the streets of Montreal.

Fortunately, it is superb weather here, and we can see this elegant capital at our ease.

All the houses have a flaunting, coquettish look, which is pleasant to see.

The streets are broad and clean.

The shops are generally very large, and very rich. There are superb goods in them. In fact, this city has a happy physiognomy, which is very agreeable.

And then one begins to find a little of the negro population, and the real American stamp peeps out, little by little. The negroes of Philadelphia are free.

We shall not meet slavery, face to face, until we leave Pennsylvania.

Be reassured, everybody! we are not going to give you any sort of dissertation on this species of American industry, any more than on these famous Quakers, with their *Basilian* hats, or these Quakeresses, sitting there so stiffly. What a change there has been since the time when these ladies exhibited themselves in open meeting, in the simple apparel, not

> "Of the beauty of a woman half-awake and half-asleep;"

but, rather, of Venus coming into the world, or of Truth climbing out of his well.

We would rather tell you about this strange sect, the Mormons, who are practicing polygamy with such success.

The number of lawful wives which is allowed

to each of these gentlemen, varies from five to twenty-four.

Five is the least that any true Mormon can put up with.

Why not the half-dozen? The Anabaptists also are addicted to this conjugal eccentricity.

But these last indulge in a little refinement.

From time to time, why, I do not know, they cut off their wives' heads!

Perhaps the Mormons will come to that in time! Have patience.

CHAPTER II.

IN WHICH EVERYBODY CATCHES A MAGNIFICENT COLD.

For the moment, the best thing we can do, I think, is to go to the Walnut street Theatre.

Mdlle. Rachel opens there this evening.

The pieces are—

LE DEPIT AND LES HORACES.

It is a hideous house, a pitiful theatre, this Walnut.

We cannot understand how so fine a city should not have something better. They are making arrangements, we are told, to build, at great expense, a house which will be really splendid.

As we have not time to wait till that is finished, we will be content, for to-night, with what we have.

We have to suffer for it; not on account of the receipts, which are very fair; not on account of the success, which is very great; but on account of its being so frightfully cold behind the scenes.

There is no fire and we are thoroughly frozen. Everybody catches cold.

Mdlle. Rachel, who, since that night at the Metropolitan, has never entirely recovered from her cough, suffers so from the cold to-night that the next day she is taken seriously ill, and is obliged to take her bed.

From this moment, until she started for Charlestown, she does not leave Jones' Hotel, where she stays with her sister Sarah.

Now begins a veritable procession of physicians, which gives rise to this lugubrious hoax of the death of Mdlle. Rachel in the Philadelphia papers.

But there is something about it which is not so easy to understand, and that is, that these papers, in their account of this unfortunate event, give the most precise details, the most minute circumstances.

So that all the newspapers in the Union vie with each other in repeating the Philadelphian pleasantry, and as the canard *(joke)* is an animal which has special facility in crossing the water, it soon reaches England and France, as a well authenticated fact.

Which, however, does not in the least prevent Mademoiselle Rachel from laughing until she weeps, when she learns that she is thoroughly dead and partially buried!

Mademoiselle Rachel's good-humor is entertained a little by the orthography and style of the following missive, which is addressed to her at Jones' Hotel, with a request that she would get it to her brother. Here it is, in all its freshness:

" *To Mr. Raphaël Félix.*

" SIR—Will you have the goodness *for* to *directed* the *tragedy* of *Adrien le Courrier to be played* on Thursday or Saturday evening or next week and not *in* Friday, because several *of* families of *the* Jews *desires* greatly *for* to see your incomparable sister Mdlle. Rachel, in this piece and *would* not go to the theater on their Sabbath. By complying with this request, you will oblige many Jews and others besides."

It is impossible for any one to be more overwhelmed than Mademoiselle Rachel, and all because she cannot play this *Adrien le Courrier* which they desire so much to applaud; but nobody is bound to perform an impossibility. She is decidedly sick, and remains imprisoned in the solemn room of her solemn hotel. To relieve the tedium of her captivity, I give her Cooper's novels, which she has not read until now. In what better place could one be than in that beautiful city, on the banks of the very Delaware, to become acquainted with the works of the great American novelist?

It is odd enough, that the sons of the New World manifest a very subdued admiration for their illustrious countryman. We expected to see statues of Cooper in all public places. Statue to an author in America! Bah! they do not even read his works! That is a literary fact. Americans do not read—they count. They find that more instructive!

CHAPTER III.

IN WHICH MILLION-HUNTING BEGINS TO BE POOR SPORT.

WHILE waiting for the health of Mademoiselle Rachel to improve, the French company and the English troupe of the Walnut Theatre give four nights.

The first night consists of

NAVAL ENGAGEMENTS,
(An English comedy,)

LES DROITS DE L'HOMME,

AND

LE PERE DE LA DEBUTANTE,
Translated into English.

This piece is very well played by M. John Sefton (the father of the debutante), and by Miss Weston, who makes a charming waiting-maid.

The 22d of November was the second night of the English and French companies.

Same programme as yesterday, with the

exception of Naval Engagements, which is replaced by

VERT VERT,

translated into English. Miss Weston plays the part created by Dejazet.

For these nights the prices are not raised, as may be supposed; the first places cost fifty cents, and the second, twenty-five. The effect of which is, that the American public which decides to come, represents very nearly the public of the Folies, or of the Delassements, and that our French pieces make the same impressions that English pieces make upon the *titis* of our minor theatres. While the French in the orchestra are applauding, the spectators in the gallery give themselves up, on their seats, to dishevelled dances with little girls, very low-necked, who have not the appearance of suffering from severe morals, and whom policemen venture to preach to a little, now and then.

These little fools are neither better nor worse than those who flaunt up and down Broadway, in New York, in broad daylight.

Regular laths, disguised as women, and

nothing else. Decidedly, America is a flat country, in every way.

During the *Droits de l'Homme* all these bedlamites make such a noise in the gallery, they imitate the cries of so many different animals, that it is a physical impossibility to hear one's self. The French in the pit call the Americans hard names, which are repaid in apple-peelings and nut shells. In fine, it is an unparalleled muss.

On the 23d, the third night,

BLUE DEVILS,

by the English Troupe.

LE MARI DE LA VEUVE,

LE CHAPEAU D'UN HORLOGER,

and lastly,

THE YOUNG WIDOW,

by Miss Weston.

On the 24th, *Tartuffe* is announced, but Mdlle. Sarah (*Elmire*) sprained her foot, and the French troupe played that night only

LE CHAPEAU D'UN HORLOGER.

The English troupe finished the performances with a grand burletta,

MASKS AND FACES.

The four nights have earned in all, and for all, 4,000 francs! at the very most!

A paltry result, which determines the administration to stop there! Decidedly, it is bad business, this playing without Rachel.

Unfortunately, she does not seem very well prepared to continue her performances! Far otherwise! She is ill! And there is talk of nothing less than of leaving the New World, and returning to France! However, there is nothing official about that. Impossible to obtain any definite answer from the administration. For a good reason, which is, that the administration does not know any more about it than other people. Everything depends on Rachel! Everything! Shall we start? Shall we stay? That is the question! At last the order comes to pack trunks, and make ready to start in the morning.

To start! very good! But where for? Europe? No! The tour is to be continued, at least in part. Mdlle. Rachel is going to Charleston; the climate is Italian there. She will recover there infallibly. There will be no playing at Baltimore, or Washington, or

Richmond, in spite of the arrangements made with these three cities.

On the 27th, at two o'clock, Mdlle. Rachel takes the railroad for Charleston; her father and her sister Sarah accompany her. The rest of the French company will take the last train.

CHAPTER IV.

A WELL-FED CANARD.

While waiting for the hour of starting, we went to visit the Fairmount water-works, the Cemetery, Girard College, and the Park.

There we were attacked by an army of little squirrels running between our legs and even trying to get up on our backs, as if we were old acquaintances.

Ah! it is not in Philadelphia as it is in Boston; no one can make the least bit of a pie of them here, and there is a fine, even for molesting them. These little animals are strangely in luck. Once, to prevent them from devouring all the maize, a price was set on their heads, and enormous sums were expended to destroy them, and now they have a park to live in and policemen to protect them!

While we are leaving these peaceful inhabitants of the Philadelphia park we see on the walls a placard deluged with exclamation points, which immediately attracts our attention. On the bill we read in immense characters—

> "ATROCIOUS MURDER!!!!!
>
> "Assassination of a mother and her nine children!!!!!
>
> "The bodies of the innocent victims have been found in the waters of the Delaware!!!!!"

Then lower down it was added (in letters which were also very prominent) that all the details of this crime would be found in a certain newspaper, the name of which I have forgotten.

You can imagine all the comments to which this placard might give rise. Some said that the husband of this poor woman had cut her throat and those of their unfortunate children.

Others, more moderate, declared there was no assassination about it, and that this woman, whom *they knew very well*, had poisoned herself. She had been so miserably poor, and had made her too numerous progeny share her suicide.

To clear up our doubts, we bought the newspaper in question soon after, and we learned at last the meaning of this gloomy enigma.

It was—it was a cat and her nine kittens that had been strangled and thrown into the river!

By means of this queer pleasantry, which set the whole city agog, and against which nobody had any right to grumble, this journal, of small circulation, was sold that day by thousands of copies!

As you see, the Philadelphia press has a very agreeable knowledge of the nature of the canard!

But it is striking twelve! Midnight! It is at this fantastic hour that the infernal machine must drag us to the South on diabolical railroads! Hurry, hurry! Start, everybody, and devil take the hindmost!

Seventh Part.

SOUTHWARD.

CHAPTER I.

IN WHICH THE RAILROADS BECOME MORE AND MORE IMPOSSIBLE.

The Americans are all very proud to tell you that they have nine hundred thousand leagues of railroads, and that, placing them one after another, there would be enough to make a girdle for the terrestrial globe!

My God! had they more than enough to make a road to the moon, that would not make them any better or safer!

We have already found that the Boston road was a miracle of headlong carelessness.

As we advance into the interior of the country, we find that they are far more extraordinary.

The grading is not solid, the bridges are temporary, thrown together in haste, built of bad timbers, which bend under the weight of the cars and seem as if they would break every minute; and all that is flung, with an audacity which has no name, right into the midst of interminable marshes, immense rivers, torrents which thunder at your feet, and immeasurable precipices; in a word, a thousand and one opportunities to break your neck, a necessity of these wild forests of North America.

And then they are so badly arranged.

When, after a great deal of trouble, you are comfortably installed in your car, *Stop!* The train stops, and you go on board another.

You must step out in the middle of the night, half asleep, and grope about to find the new train which you have to take, and which is always a very long way from that which you have just left.

Not a man to tell you the way or show you.

That is precisely what happens to us in Baltimore, where we get out just in the middle of a street, at two o'clock in the morning, straightway to climb into another car.

We are scarcely asleep in our new quarters—caring very little, in this dark night, to catch the least glimpse of the capital of Maryland—when we are compelled to get out again to take a steamboat which was waiting for us with steam up.

This time, we hope that we can rest in full security.

Mistaken! Five minutes afterwards we leave the boat for a third railroad, and at day-break, at Washington, we leave this third rail-road for a second steamboat. What a life!

After having dallied down the Potomac, a very pretty river, *ma foi!* which separates Maryland from Virginia, and which is literally covered with ducks, we land at Fredericks-burg.

There we recommence our railroad amuse-ment, and at two o'clock in the afternoon we take an indifferent breakfast at Richmond, the capital of Virginia.

Two hours afterward we dine in Petersburg, where we change cars, to keep up the habit, and at last, at nine o'clock at night, we arrive at Weldon, tired, worn out, half dead, and there,

O happy lot! we remain in the arms of this swindler, Morpheus, till next morning. We did not cheat him.

Say what you will, this perpetual travelling has an attraction which cannot be denied, a charm which you cannot help feeling. Positively this eternal locomotion produces a real intoxication. For us the seasons are no more. Winter, autumn, spring, summer, all come at present, without order. Yesterday we were covered with furs like genuine Esquimaux, to-morrow we shall be dressed in white linen. For myself, I know not how I am living. To find what month it is, I have to refer to my almanac. People must go mad very easily in this country!

CHAPTER II.

IN WHICH THERE IS TALK ABOUT THE SON OF LOUIS XVI.

Next morning we received by telegraph very good news from Mdlle. Rachel, who is coming on by short trips, and who, although she started long before us, will not be in Weldon until several hours after our departure.

We do not leave until noon. We have, then, more time than we need, to look about a little in this rather rough country, where we have to stay a quarter of an hour.

One of our travelling companions, a strapping New Orleans merchant, nothing else! offers to be our guide in the little excursion which we feel compelled to make.

We enthusiastically accept, and, in a little while, step on the banks of a beautiful river, under grand trees draped with ivy, a few steps from a magnificent waterfall, which pours roaring upon a rock and leaps up again so as to spatter us, a truly picturesque site, which brings to mind the novels of this Cooper, of whom we were speaking a moment ago. Had there been a few savages to animate it, the scene would have been complete!

Scarcely had we said a few words about Cooper, his novels and these savage tribes, half exterminated, when our guide, the Louisianian, began to tell us, without any high-flown phrases, I assure you, and without aiming at all at effect, a story, or rather a legend, which he had once heard in Albany, and which is so odd, so inconceivable, and so fantastic, that I should hardly dare to repeat it here, had I not found it in full in a remarkable work of M. Ampère on the New World.*

M. Ampère did not see, with his own eyes, the individual in question, but he has all the details from a man perfectly well known in the United States, Mr. J. C. Spencer, a distinguished advocate and celebrated counsellor-at-law, whose veracity cannot be called in question.

We will therefore substitute, if you please,

* *Promenades en Amerique,* Michel Levi freres.

the story of M. Spencer, as M. Ampère gives it in his book, for that of our friend the Louisianian.

"There is now living in the city of Albany, when he is not busy preaching to some Indian tribes, still remaining at Green Bay, near Lake Michigan, a minister of the Methodist persuasion. His name is Eleazer Williams; he is precisely of the age which the last dauphin would have been, and is said to bear a striking resemblance both to Louis XVI. and to Marie Antoinette. This Williams was brought up by an Indian named Williams, from whom he derived his name, and who passed for his father; but who was not. So at least Williams's wife has always declared. Besides, the name of this supposed child cannot be found on the register, where the births of the rest of Williams's children are recorded.

"Some years ago, there died in New Orleans a Frenchman, whose name was Bellanger. On his deathbed, he declared that the dauphin had been rescued from the Temple; that another child had been substituted, and that, terror-stricken at the revolutionary ideas of Citizen

Genet, one of the most violent representatives of the French Republic, he had taken the boy away to the Indians and confided him to the care of Williams.

"As to Eleazer Williams, he has no remembrance of his early years. (It has been said, that the hideous treatment of Simon injured the intellect of his innocent victim.) The Methodist preacher has a vague recollection that he was once seated on the knees of a lady, around whom were powdered heads and epaulettes. With that exception, he remembers nothing of all his life, until a certain day when, while he was swimming in a lake with some young Indians, he hit his head against a rock. From that moment his memory is distinct. He asserts that a Frenchman, who came among the savages with whom he was living, said once, pointing him out, 'This is a king's son.'

"His education was paid for, very promptly, in college, by the Indian Williams, who, like all half-civilized savages, was a great brandy-drinker, never had a cent, and gave no education to his real children.

"Williams's widow had in her possession a

bronze medal, on which was represented the marriage of Louis XVI. to Marie Antoinette. She used to say that her husband had had two others of the same, one gold and the other silver, and that he had sold them for drink, and she saved this, the third one.

" In certain memoirs of the time (I have not verified the quotation), it is stated that one day Simon, in one of those brutal fits to which he was subject, struck the dauphin on the face with a napkin, and the nail on which it was hanging, and which he tore out in snatching it down, wounded the nose of the victim in two places. Eleazer Williams has scars in these two places.

" While autographs were once being shown him, without allowing him to see the signatures, at the sight of one he was struck with horror, and a sort of shuddering: it was the hand-writing of Simon!

" Finally, when the Prince de Joinville was in the United States, he went out of his way to see Williams, who was then among the Indians in the neighborhood of Green Bay. They had several hours' conversation; Williams refuses to tell what passed between them. Only this, he speaks very highly of the Prince, who has since sent him books.

"The most curious circumstance of this strange story is the answer of Williams when he is asked what he thinks of it all:

"'Really,' says he, 'this assemblage of circumstances is very striking: I do not know how to explain it; but there is one thing certain; I do not want to be king.'

"This last peculiarity distinguishes him at any rate from the adventurers who have claimed that they were sons of Louis XVI., and ought to satisfy everybody—at least, all whom this story convinces—that they should hunt up this Methodist preacher at Albany or among his savages and make him king in spite of himself!"

While listening to this strange story, this legend told there under those gigantic trees, beside this torrent which was roaring at my feet, I admit that I experienced a strange emotion; a thousand memories arose, and as if in a dream, it seemed to me that all these memories of the past century were alive again and passing before me!

At this moment the railroad bell rang for starting. The big Louisianian, astonished at the effect which he had produced, struck me on the shoulder, and two minutes afterward we were leaving Weldon at full speed!

CHAPTER III.

IN WHICH MAY BE SEEN FEMALE VAMPIRES AND BIRDS OF PREY.

After having passed a horrible night in Wilmington, a hideous little city of North Carolina, we arrive at last, on the first of December, at five o'clock in the morning, without any sort of accident, at Charleston in South Carolina.

This city is dreadfully filthy; besides, it is very ugly, and outrageously built!

We are now in the midst of slavery. One cannot walk a step without setting his foot on a negro.

They are very polite, these same negroes, here. When they pass a *bon blanc*, they bow to him! So that the *bon blanc*, taken by surprise, fancies that these sham chimney-sweeps are acquainted with him, and he is ready to return their bow, and commence a conversation! Which would be very scandalous! I beg you to believe it!

For the rest, these slaves do not seem unhappy at all! They are gayer than in New York, where they are as free as if they were in the woods—as you know.

Here they are always laughing! As to the negresses, if they can always have an enormous culotted pipe in their mouths, it is all they want! These fine women smoke from morning till night; it is their habit, their hobby, their rage!

And they are ugly with those horrid instruments between their lips! They are!

One thing is charming—the temperature which we have here! Real spring weather. Everywhere, in the gardens, in the streets, even, we see roses in bloom, orange trees covered with fruit! It is delightful!

What is not delightful may be seen, any morning, by the shore.

There the garbage of the city is thrown, and it is the rendezvous of fifty or sixty old negresses, half-naked, with skinny limbs, hooked fingers, long, white teeth, and little eyes, like to those of fallow deer.

It is a disgusting sight. Real ghouls' heads! The female vampires of the Arabian Nights.

These old monsters, with their fingers, rake over heaps of ordure, and pick out what seems to them eatable, or worth taking.

To complete the picture, big red-headed vultures flutter around these old sorcerers, dig with them in the uncleanness, and swallow, in enormous pieces, the putrefied bodies of dead animals!

It is all pure barbarism!

CHAPTER IV.

IN WHICH YOU ARE INTRODUCED TO A NEW SAINT.

While waiting for this beautiful Charleston climate to restore thoroughly the health of Mdlle. Rachel, Raphaël takes the steamer Isabel for the island of Cuba, in order to make the necessary preparations for the performances of the great tragédienne in Havana.

On the 10th of December—that is to say, several days after the departure of its director—the French company plays in the theatre at Charleston. The pieces are:

LE DEPIT AMOUREUX.
LES DROITS DE L'HOMME.
LE CHAPEAU D'UN HORLOGER.

The receipts threatened, for a time, not to be bad; but, unhappily, on the opening of the office, a formidable fire broke out near by. And, by our lady! we are not afraid to repeat it, fires are one of the *grandes passions* of the American people! *Panem et incendia!* This is the cry of these ultra-marine Romans!

And, besides, they have it always in their mouths. It is monstrous what a quantity of houses they burn in this country. So many, that, in certain cities of the Union, if a single day should pass without a fire, the people would be more dissatisfied than they could possibly be at anything else.

"No fire!" they would say to each other, with a shudder; "what's the meaning of it?"

People of the country (with shrewish tongues, doubtless) say that, from time to time, merchants who are in bad circumstances set fire to their warehouses with their own hands!

As they are all insured for very handsome sums, they get their insurance, and set themselves afloat again, as if nothing had happened.

There are people, too, who say (mere calumny, we doubt not) that sometimes the insurance companies themselves burn a few houses, to frighten people who know no better, and so get more business

It is, of course, to be understood that the

company which indulged in this description of speculation, never burns houses insured by itself, but always those insured by a rival company, which in a few days returns the compliment; and this is perfectly logical. Moreover, nobody has the courage to find fault with them for it. People are so fond of fires.

So, this evening, listen to these joyous shouts, these bells which are ringing so gaily, these songs of joy! It is a real fête for Charleston; to-day is *St. Fire!*

Four houses devoured by the flames! Te Deum, four houses! A good windfall! If they had had six, they would have had an illumination! Well, they will next time.

Three days after this half failure, we gave

TARTUFFE.

Tartuffe,	MM.	Chéry, aîné.
Orgon,	"	Bellevaut.
Valère,	"	Léon Beauvallet.
Cléante,	"	Latouche.
Damis,	"	Dieudonné.
Loyale,	"	Pelletier.
L'Exempt,	"	Chéry, jeune.
Elmire,	Mdlles.	Sarah Félix.
Marianne,	"	Lia Félix.
Dorine,	"	Dinah Félix.
Mme. Pernelle,	"	Durrey.

As we gave tickets to all the cooks at our hotels, and as these cooks are all French, the piece had a stunning success. As great, if not greater, than

ADRIENNE LECOUVREUR,

which was played on the 17th of December by RACHEL. Yes, by Rachel. She is not quite well; she still has this accursed cough, which will not leave her; but, at last, she resolves to play in spite of it, and she does play!

Unfortunately, she plays to-night *for the last time* in America.

On the bills the public are notified that Rachel would give *one* night—a *single* night—and that *positively*. The management did not think that it was speaking so truly!

CHAPTER V.

IN WHICH WE EMBARK FOR THE WEST INDIES.

During these performances, the Isabel returned from Havana, with letters from Raphaël.

Business is going on very well down there. There are a good many subscribers. The chest is getting heavy with piastres.

The best thing to do, therefore, is to embark immediately, on this same steamer Isabel, and join the director, Raphaël Félix, in Cuba. That is what we do.

The captain puts his state-room very gallantly at the disposition of Mdlle. Rachel and Mdlle. Sarah, who eagerly accept it, as it is on deck and better than any of the others.

On the nineteenth, at ten o'clock in the morning, the Isabel leaves the port of Charleston. The next day we steam along the coast of Georgia; we stop awhile before Savannah, the capital of that same Georgia, to take on board more passengers, and a few hours afterwards we came coasting along Florida, where there are now six thousand Indians, in a state of insurrection, against whom the United States have just sent several regiments. Towards night we see a grove of palms in flames. It is one of the signals of the Indians.

This country is exceedingly convenient for that. You wish to notify a friend that you are in any place, no matter where · you set a forest on fire and it tells the whole story. On the 21st of December, the Isabel landed at Key West, a little port in Florida, inhabited only by pirates, negroes, and savages.

With the desire simply, I suppose, of seeing these slightly picturesque hosts close by, Mdlle. Rachel, who decidedly does not manifest any foolish gayety as she approaches the tropics, consents, for the first time since coming on board, to cross the threshold of the captain's state-room. Still more, O prodigious event! She ventured, on the arm of that same captain, and surrounded by her numerous family, to make a sort of journey to an admirable grove, *ma foi!* a regular hot-house, particularly hot, where palms and cocoa trees grow as if they were at home, and cactuses flourish with frightful facility. There the promegranate opens of itself to your thirst; the lemon falls ripe into your—mouth; there humming-birds replace our cock-chafers; butterflies are as big as warming pans, and grasshoppers sing opera airs.

When you find yourself suddenly face to face with this luxuriant nature, you feel that *something has not yet happened.* Indeed, it has just the same effect upon you as a fifth act of a fairy play.

While the Félix family are promenading among these robust plants, the other members of the French Company profit by the opportunity to wander about on the shore.

It is very moist—this beach—and besides it is ornamented with sponges, shells which are alive, and snakes which are still more alive.

The proof of which is, that one of these last, wishing, probably, to poke a few sticks in the wheels of the Félix enterprise, leaps upon several tragedians present, and endeavors to devour them.

He must have a tragedian—this serpent—

there is no use in mincing the matter! the gourmand!

Randoux does not lose his presence of mind; and with a voice which silenced the sound of the waves, he commenced the recital of Theramenes.

He was hardly half through before the snake was sound asleep.

By the effect which this scrap of literature produces upon him, we very readily recognize in this ophidian a citizen of the United States!

We treacherously took advantage of his slumbers to deluge him with blows, and "when he awoke he was dead."

(I have been asked lately if this was a matter of history, and if, in very fact, tragedy has this effect on snakes in Florida. Let the inquirer consult the first herpetologist who comes along, and see what he will say!)

After this exploit, or this assassination, just as you please, we go back to the steamer, which, without loss of time, carries us far away from this country, so truly fantastic and absolutely miraculous—with the exception of the snakes!

The next day, in a magnificent sunrise, we enter the admirable harbor of Havana, under full steam, where we are received with firing of cannon. This is captivating.

One thing is funny enough; all the vessels in the harbor are transformed into clothes-lines.

On the masts, on the yards—everywhere, you see waistcoats drying in the sun, and pantaloons polking with the wind.

This time, at least, no serenade will be spoiled, like that at New York; and for a very good reason—nobody here dreams of giving the least bit of a serenade to the great *tragédienne!*

Mdlle. Rachel, therefore, lands in the midst of a perfectly tranquil population, who have the good taste not to weary the illustrious traveller by tedious acclamations.

Eighth Part.

THE QUEEN OF THE ANTILLES.

CHAPTER I.

IN WHICH PEOPLE SPEAK SPANISH AT EVERY STEP.

THE Queen of the Antilles!—a pretty name and a charming country, certainly!

To say that at Philadelphia, at Charleston, even, at two steps from this *Bella-Habana* (ah! faith, English is buried now; we are going to commit ourselves to ferocious Spanish!) to say that we had failed, had retreated, were thoroughly routed away!

We should never have got over that!

With what depth of joy, therefore, with what unspeakable pleasure, we handed our passports to the Havana police! For one must show his passports here; it is not exactly as it is in the United States!

The officers above-named appear very well, and they are exquisitely polite. They call you "Seigneur!" every moment, as in tragedies. That is flattering! And so you give, without much regret, to these gentlemen, these *Señores*, I should say (let us speak Castilian!) the moderate sum of two *pesos* (the dollar of the place), in exchange for *una boleta de desembarco;* or, if you prefer it, a permit of disembarkation.

For the matter of trunks and valises, we had been told in New York that they would rake everything here from top to bottom; that they would confiscate our arms, appropriate our soap, and lay a heavy hand on our pomades! Calumny! Pure calumny! The custom-house is less rigid here than anywhere else; the officers scarcely glance at our baggage; which allows us, thank God, soon to make our definite entrée into this city, for which we are sighing so, and which has so little resemblance—I am saying nothing against it now—to the other cities of North America.

One thing which strikes us immediately, is to see soldiers, genuine soldiers!

For, in the United States, the soldier, properly speaking, has no existence, and here he exists, only too fully developed.

His uniform is very simple; blue striped kersey pantaloons, blouse of the same, confined at the waist by a belt of buff-skin, and a broad-brimmed straw hat.

However, as all the Havana soldiers are tall fellows, with bronzed complexions and black mustaches, their uniform, though not extravagantly rich, does not fail to produce, on their backs, a striking effect.

In the streets you meet them at every step—and negroes, too!

As to the Señores, Señoras, and Señoritas, God forbid that they should ever set their aristocratic feet on the very rough, very slippery, and very filthy pavement of the capital of the island of Cuba! They would all prefer being chopped into mince-meat to going out any other way than in a *volante*—a sort of chaise holding two or three, stuck on two enormous wheels, endowed with two thills prodigiously long, and driven, à la Daumont, by a negro more or less naked.

The volante is immensely important here; it is almost impossible to do without it.

Those who have none, invite themselves to one when they choose, by means of—a *peseta*, or two reals, the trip (20 cents).

The number of these carriages in Havana is incredible; and this is very inconvenient for foot-passengers, as the streets are exceedingly narrow, the sidewalks almost imperceptible, and you have to take all the pains in the world to keep your bones from being broken under the gigantic, perpetual-motion wheels of these bedevilled vehicles.

At last, by taking some precautions, we reach the gates of the city, which are watched night and day by the soldiery.

There we see old fortifications, half-ruined, covered with ivy, and very picturesque.

It is needless to say that the vegetation here is as fairy-like as in Florida. What am I saying? Still more so; for we are now right under the tropic, just in the same latitude (if my geographical notions do not deceive me) as the great desert of Sahara, another place not very cool, where one can see camels hatched!

CHAPTER II.

IN WHICH IT IS A GREAT DEAL HOTTER THAN IN AN OVEN!

As to the city, it has a little peculiarity, half Spanish and half Moorish, which must not be overlooked.

Nearly all the houses are painted blue, or pink, or yellow; that is jolly enough. And then you have every facility for seeing the sky here! The houses are generally nothing but a basement, rarely a first story! As to windows, they are out of the question! You cannot have too much air! Every *casa* has simply large openings furnished with iron gratings, which makes one think, at first, that the city is only a vast collection of butchers' shops!

All the houses are built on this plan. Even the rich hotels of the *cerro*. Which does not prevent the parlors on the level of the street from being truly magnificent. One thing is rather curious—these same parlors often serve to house the *volante*. A carriage in a room—that is an idea! Why not the horses, too?

Instead of the horses, you can see under these gilded mouldings and this rich furniture, flocks of hens and chickens, ducks and ducklings. It is not, however, for the benefit of their conversation that these estimable fowls are received so well in Havana families; no, not that.

Only, as they have a talent in the way of destroying worms, crickets, scorpions, and other insects, nobody hesitates to receive them.

Thanks to the absent windows, you see all this indoor life without any trouble at all; you see, carelessly stretched on their reed chairs, all these charming little Creoles, with childish hands, invisible feet, large eyes, splendid hair, and always in ball dress.

Ball dress is the ordinary costume of ladies in Havana, morning and night, winter and summer.

While they are gently poising themselves in their arm-chairs, they twirl in their fingers a cigarette which they have half smoked.

When their large eyes close, their little

fingers drop the unfinished cigar, and all these Señoras hasten on a little trip to dream-land.

Dreams! People must dream here! They are always asleep! At a certain hour of the day, when this blackguard Phœbus is firing away at the hottest, Havana is no longer Havana; it is the palace of the Beauty of the Sleeping Forest.

At this hour of compulsory slumber, the gentleman who is so young as to fall in love, sinks to sleep while saying to his Señorita, "I love you," and she replies by an adorable yawn.

The merchant snores on his counter, and the customer who understands himself, takes an arm-chair and a nap by his side.

In the streets, under the palms of the *Paseo*, at the doors of the houses, everybody goes to sleep.

The animals themselves cannot escape the general drowsiness.

The horse stops gradually, and at last moves neither hand nor foot; the dog can no longer bark at the cat, who rubs her tail in his eye as she passes, and who, herself, prefers laying down in the dust, to taking the trouble even of reaching out her paw to a mouse who is nibbling at two steps from her, and who is so overpowered by the heat, that he has not even the courage to be afraid and run away.

CHAPTER III.

IN WHICH THE BEDS ARE NOT SO SOFT AS THEY MIGHT BE.

While waiting for the touch of the wand, which transforms Havana into a vast bed-room, we go to breakfast at Legrand's restaurant on the Paseo.

Legrand is a Frenchman, and I present him my compliments therefor; his cuisine is also French, and I felicitate him more and more; only his prices seemed to me a little too Spanish.

There, at this same Legrand's, Mdlle. Rachel stopped with her father and her three sisters.

Raphaël Félix alone takes no part in this family party; he stays with a friend.

Mdlle. Rachel goes to her rooms. In her bed-room she perceives, with horror, that the bed which is destined for her is nothing but a hammock bed.

A hammock bed for Hermione! for Camille! for Phœdra! Impossible! However, it is true!

And on this hammock bed not a shadow of a straw mattress, not a suspicion of a hair mattress. Two small sheets are all in all!

That is the only extra that one can indulge in, it is so hot!

And here we are at the end of December! It must be comfortable here in August!

Mdlle. Rachel does not trouble herself much about all that; she must have a mattress. Just as, at Philadelphia, she must have the milk of a white donkey. There was no white donkey in Philadelphia; so one had to be made to order for her!

And here pursuit is made of a mattress maker! A mattress maker at Havana! it is a rarity, a phenomenon!

At last, after pursuing him under some thousands of difficulties, he is found, and the great tragédienne gets her mattress! In five minutes nothing else was spoken of in the whole city! It was worth the trouble, *pardieu,* just for that!

We make our way through the knots of people, who assemble at the corners of the streets to talk over this great event, and establish ourselves in the Hotel de L'Union, No. 110 Calle de O'Reilly! an excellent house, in fact, the best in the city, according to connoisseurs, kept by Bernard, a very pleasant fellow, a Frenchman, whom everybody in the city knows, and who knows everybody in the city, and shakes hands regularly from a hundred to a hundred and fifty times, every time he ventures his nose in the street.

The great tragédienne was to have stopped at Bernard's; but Legrand carried off the palm!

Lucky Legrand!

The Hotel Bernard is literally crammed with travellers. A private room is an impossibility. But a single one is now vacant. Fortunately that is a large one. Randoux, Dieudonné and I take possession of it. In the matter of furniture it has three beds, hammock beds, of course, with musquito nets.

The musquito net is indispensable here; for without it one would be devoured from the hair to the sole of the feet.

Unfortunately, it sometimes happens that a musquito finds means to make his way under the gauze; and *ma foi!* when he is once there, this interesting animal without any backbone, (for it is an established fact that musquitoes have no backbones,) has but one thing to do—to gnaw upon you all night!

These three hammock beds cost us, for the three, the mere bagatelle of 950 francs a month ($180). Really, that is not dear; true, we have to pay extra for our washing.

It is understood, of course, that meals are included in this price for hammock beds. And the eating is excellent at the hotel Bernard. How different from that odious American cuisine.

Here the very sight of the table has something pleasant about it.

In fact, you see here real bottles of wine, genuine bread, and authentic napkins! three things totally unknown in the United States.

After dinner, under the escort of this same Bernard, we take a ride to the *Cerro* and *Las Pucntes*, charming promenades planted with palms and cocoa trees with immense tops. Nothing is so delicious as to lounge about in this way of an evening, in the country, discussing a delightfully dreamy cigar, fresh, and retaining all its aroma. When they are half gray (for these cigars turn gray admirably), we come to the *Campo Santo* of the city, the cemetery, if you like that better.

Here there is a magnificent echo, and we talk with the departed! Really the effect is fantastic; one would say that this voice which is repeating our sentences, our words, our syllables, arose from one of these tombs which we see there in the moonlight! for there is a splendid moon to-night, without which the scene would not have been brought out well. Myriads of stars are sparkling in the skies, invisible insects fill the air with a strange harmony. In the grass of the meadows, and on the sand of the road, thousands of glowworms are creeping, leaving behind them a phosphorescent track! On the bushes, in the trees, everywhere innumerable cucullos are fluttering, real live diamonds! which seem to have been created expressly to illuminate this wonderful tropical evening.

CHAPTER IV.

IN WHICH TOO MANY GLASSES BEGIN TO BE TAKEN.

Returning to the city, we step into the ball of the *Paseo.* A very noisy ball, indeed, from which Mdlle. Rachel is separated only by a single wall.

She hears the squalling orchestra of this dancing establishment, as plainly as if she were right in the midst of the dancers!

So that she cannot sleep to-night, and already begins to think of making her escape from the *Casa del Señor Legrand.*

It is horrible for her, as you may well suppose, what with being sick, having to lie on mattresses obtained with great difficulty, and to hear by the side of her room a crowd of fools jumping about, to the discordant noise of four equivocal fiddles and half a dozen cornets à piston.

We rescue ourselves very quickly from this

unwholesome place, and hasten to the Place d'Armes, a charming spot, I declare, covered with magnificent trees, plants which are seen nowhere else, and flowers whose names, even, you do not know.

And all that is lighted with gas! O civilization.

Under the Captain-General's windows a military band gives a concert every night, which never fails to attract an audience as select as it is numerous.

At this hour, everybody in Havana wakes up, the young ladies dress, as if for a ball, and drive, in splendid volantes and charming little carriages, to the chosen rendezvous.

Most of them remain in their equipages, where, voluptuously reclining on their velvet cushions, they listen less to the concert, than to the flatteries of young hidalgos, who come cooing to their feet!

But the palace-bell is striking nine! It is the signal for breaking up.

In an instant the place is deserted!

Let us follow the crowd, and go to take a punch or lemonade with them, to the splendid

Diana or *Dominica* saloon, while our little creoles, still in their volantes, are served, at the door, with some refreshment or other!

From this moment, there commences a sort of refrain, which pursues you incessantly, and without relaxation, in the street, at the theatre, in the country, at the bath! It is your shadow, your nightmare, your double! This haunting refrain is: "Shall we take a glass!"

To tell you the number of glasses which a man is compelled to take here, is a thing which cannot be done! Enough to drown you!

But it is getting late; you have here, I believe, a day tolerably well employed; the Hotel Bernard claims us; our hammock beds stretch out their arms to us; let us go to sleep!

CHAPTER V.

IN WHICH THE SUNDAYS ARE NOT LIKE UNITED STATES SUNDAYS.

To sleep—it is easy to say, but terribly hard to do! I am not speaking now of musquitoes—they are nothing; we are acclimated, and pay no attention to them; but the ants—the deuce! they are quite another thing! I'faith, I have no sort of hatred for these little animals. But, under the pretense that they have the infatuation of living together socially, like bees, as M. Buffon says, that is no reason why they should fix the seat of their society in my bed. It is very true that, if these excellent economists were not my nocturnal companions, that would not prevent me from hearing the roulades of two young mulattresses, who live in the next house. Ah! why are they not at the conservatory! Thank God! they are still! and now we can——

At the very moment in which we are closing our weary eyes, two or three cats, aroused, probably, by the flourishes of the mulattresses, began to make a racket—a racket loud enough to frighten a deaf man. A horse, which has his quarters in the court of this unorganized menagerie, irritated, apparently, by this noise, began to snort and neigh; another animal, which I took, for a long time, to be a pig, but which, really, was nothing but an asthmatic sheep, avails himself of this opportunity to perform his part in this ridiculous concert; meantime, add the monotonous cry of the *serenos* (watchmen), who announce, every minute, to the inhabitants, what o'clock it is, and are laughed at for their pains, and you will have, precisely, our first night in the West Indies. Fortunately, it was not long before daybreak.

All the better that to-day is Sunday! Thank heaven, this day is not spent here as in the United States! Very differently!

Among the thousand amusements which one can indulge in to-day, in Havana, the cock-fights are the most curious and exciting.

These come off in a little street outside of the city. A sort of small circus, built of boards, with three galleries, serves as a theatre for these strange combats. There, every Sunday, incalculable sums are bet, gained, and lost. It is the *bourse* of the place. For bustle it has no reason to envy the *bourse* of Paris.

At the time of our entrance a fight is just over. All the betters, dripping with sweat and half-naked, have jumped into the pit and are settling their bets, not without shouts and gesticulations, I assure you.

But the commissioner rings his bell and all these people quit the arena. Another fight is about to commence. No one remains in the pit except the commissioner and the owners of the cocks which are going to tear each other in pieces, and which are at last flown at each other!

The two cocks first measure each other with their eye; then, after a few feints, they leap up to it with a courage and a ferocity which is indescribable. They aim only at the head, especially at the eyes, and give each other atrocious wounds; they are nearly always blind before the end of the fight. When the tussle begins to slacken, each owner seizes his limping bird and washes his wings. Then he refreshes him by blowing over him a little brandy and water.

The two champions, but just now half-dead, are flown at each other anew, and they begin afresh the work of mutual laceration! Then new bets are made; furious yells shake the circus; people get up on the seats; everybody makes an effort, and the betters cheer on the combatants with mad shouts!

"Courage!" says one of those near me to the animal on which he is betting, "come, come, aim at his head! Bravo! You have hit him; another *such* blow and you will be the victor!" And, in fact, as if he had understood what this man said to him, the cock gives a finishing blow with his beak to the bloody head of his adversary, who falls on his side, flapping his wings, and dies in a moment or two. The victor then leaps upon the body of his victim, gives him two or three parting pecks in the eyes, and sets up a long crow of triumph.

There are also other fights, in which the cocks have steel spurs fitted to their legs. They hit skulls and bellies with marvellous dexterity, but that is too soon over; then you see nothing but blood! Altogether these animals are hideous *canaille;* that is my opinion!

CHAPTER VI.

IN WHICH THE FELIX ENTERPRISE FLAPS ONLY ONE WING.

On leaving the cock-fights we go to the *Plaza de Toros*, in the hope of seeing different fights, a little more dramatic; unfortunately, all the bulls are sick, and their exercises are supplied by lively and animated equestrian performances. We console ourselves by passing the evening at the *Gran Teatro de Tacon*, where the play to-night is, La Catalina, the celebrated Spanish opera, as the bill says. It is simply a literal translation of L'Etoile du Nord. The piece is carefully brought out, however, and produces a good effect.

The little drum scene had a truly enthusiastic success.

Aha! one of these young rattlers is none other than *Rosa Espert*, who came to Paris not long ago, and who is adored in Havana. She is well worth it, by heavens!

Before leaving the Tacon Theatre, we will say that it is beyond all the praise we have ever heard of it. It is a splendid house; no house in Paris can equal it.

Really, when one sees, two thousand leagues away, in half savage countries, theatres so fine, so spacious, and so comfortable, one cannot comprehend how they can endure in Paris such mean and disagreeable houses!

At the bottom of the bill of the Tacon Theatre, we see the following spectacle announced:

HORACIO.

Heigho! how quickly one guessed that meant HORACE! What a fine language, this Spanish! HORACIO!

Will they play it? Will they not play it? That is what everybody is asking, and nobody answers.

Ah! if that depended on Raphaël alone, I think the problem would not be long solving; but Mdlle. Rachel has not yet fixed the day of her first performance. Every new physician that she consults, considers himself under obligation to order her not to go on the boards again for as long a time as possible; one of these gentlemen even sincerely advised her to rest for six months at least. He thinks that then she may, without danger, begin her performances at Havana! Six months! Why not six years? Unhappily, all these people have ended in actually convincing her that she is a great deal worse than she really is, and the unfortunate performances are all the while in suspense, and expenses are running up more and more, and the public is getting impatient, and *la Prensa de Habana*, the most influential newspaper of the place, which knows that Mdlle. Rachel played some days ago in Charleston—*la Prensa*, which does not more than half believe in all this sickness, and which, consequently, discovers that Mdlle. Rachel is treating rather cavalierly these poor Havanese, who have nothing to reproach themselves for, so far as she is concerned—amuses itself by publishing, in very skillful Spanish, the biography of Mdlle. Rachel, by M. E. de Mirecourt.

All that is not exactly suited to curing her—not by a good deal! So much so, that some days after her establishment in the Hotel Legrand, she announces to her family that *M. Jorain*, the thirtieth or fortieth physician consulted by her, positively forbids her to play before the 10th of January (why not the 11th?), and that till then she must live alone, away from the bustle of a hotel, and particularly distant from the Paseo ball!

After that there was a great row in the Félix family. But what was to be done? From this instant, I am quite sure, Raphaël was perfectly convinced that it was all over.

And now that there are already fifty thousand francs of subscription in the money bags, fifty thousand francs which he must pay back to people who have taken the trouble to bring it themselves! Fatality! fatality! But there is nothing to be said, it must be done! Raphaël perceives that, he feels it, and yet, in spite of all, he still has hopes! And no notice appears in the papers, announcing to the murmuring public that the performance of the great tragédienne will not take place!

Meantime, he makes propositions to his artistes, which are received like a dog in a tenpin alley. Of course, the matter in hand was a suspension of the engagements.

Which compels him next day to come himself and make propositions which were a little more acceptable, and the artistes (who are, after, all not big children, as Mdlle. Rachel says, but very good children), ended by signing all that they were asked to, that is to say:

1st. Suspension of salary from December 26th.

2nd. Three dollars (fifteen francs) a-day, until January 20th, 1856, for current expenses.

3rd. Full reimbursement of salary, in case Mdlle. Rachel resumes the course of her performances.

Which causes everybody to make ardent vows that the performances aforesaid may resume their course in the shortest possible time.

No one, however, can desire it more ardently than Raphaël.

In fact, if he does not play, he must pay an enormous forfeiture to M. Marty, the manager of the Tacon Theatre. There is talk about writs already. And, faith, that is a serious matter here! And dear, too! Besides, this M. Marty is not exceedingly accommodating, if all I hear be true! Although, on matters of business, no one ever had occasion to find fault with him, in the least.

It is odd enough that Mdlle. Rachel goes to live in a house belonging to this same M. Marty, who is just on the point of arresting her brother.

For she follows her physician's orders to the letter, and on the very next day leaves the Hotel Legrand, never to return!

From this moment she becomes almost invisible. Aside from the visits of her too numerous physicians, she receives very few. She is cloistered in the elegant mansion of the manager of the Tacon Theatre, where even her sisters make very short calls. At last, one evening, I succeed in seeing her, and having a conversation with her. She tells me that she is getting better. In fact, she does not seem to me to be really sick. Her countenance is not changed at all, and although, from time to time, she coughs a little, one is strongly inclined to ask why she condemns herself so obstinately to this voluntary seclusion.

In fact, she speaks with me this evening, about future performances, and seems absolutely decided to play on the tenth of January, as already mentioned.

I make haste to carry this piece of good news to Raphaël, who does not receive it with the enthusiasm which I was expecting; but shakes his head, with an air which seems to say: When she plays in Havana it will be a great deal warmer than this! This movement of the directorial head was a flash of light for me, and, from that night, I began to pack my trunks.

CHAPTER VII.

LA NOCHE BUENA.

It is well said, that it is a sad and solemn thing to make preparations for a journey!

Especially, when it is to leave Havana!

Havana! this continual sunbeam, this perpetual concert, this everlasting festival!

So stop a moment; to-night, too, the whole city has an air of perfect jubilation, one of those physiognomies which it is a pleasure to see, and which can be met with only here!

In the streets, under the palms of the Paseo, innumerable troops of minstrels are coming (black or white, as you prefer), all decorated with the traditional guitar—you know, the genuine Spanish guitar (there are some left yet!).

And what are these joyous troubadours singing?

The wonders of *La Noche Buena*, of the good night—of Christmas night, in fact!

Call it what you will, Christmas night, good night, or *Noche Buena*, this festival is, undoubtedly, one of the largest, gayest, and, especially, one of the noisiest, in the whole Havana Calendar.

The bells actually enjoy it. What a charivari! What a bustle! You would say that this merry city had become the universal rendezvous of all the tinkers and sauce-pan menders of the five parts of the earth!

This is not a pleasantry, at any rate; these poor Havana bells have an impossible way of making a noise.

It is quite true that they are not *rung*. A Superior Order, I am told, forbids that. They have only the right to beat them underneath with a hammer, or a club, *ad libitum*. Which produces a peculiar sound, slightly dissonant, and rather noisy, which has a way of irritating your nervous ,system magnificently. You would say that they were cutting cork in your ears, or sticking a feather in your nose!

But it is midnight; the best thing we can do

is to go to see the numerous churches in the capital. All are splendidly illuminated.

Thousands of women, black, white, yellow, chocolate, café au lait, of all shades, in fine, most of them sparkling with jewelry and half-drowned under waves of laces, with their heads bare, of course (the bonnet is unknown here), are kneeling pell-mell, without distinction of rank, race, or color, on the pavement of the church. (Generally these ladies take the precaution to bring little carpets.)

We had heard a great deal of the piety of the Spanish ladies. We must frankly acknowledge that it did not appear to us as austere as we had been given to understand it was. But there are so many young, lively cavaliers saying soft things to them! And then it will soon be supper time!

Aha! Supper time! That is a scene which is played here without cessation!

To-night nobody will go to bed before six in the morning!

And all these people eat, drink, laugh, sing, dance, shout, yell, and behave, so that the deuce himself would take up arms at it!

Ah! I know now why, in Havana, this night is called THE GOOD NIGHT! What a Punchinello life!

CHAPTER VIII.

IN WHICH THE BIRDS MAKE THEMSELVES HAPPY.

At daybreak, for the mere sake of resting a little, Bernard, some friends, and I, take a boat, a charming little boat, *à la Venitienne*, which we load with eatables; we cross the bay and install ourselves on a green hill, shaded by trees which were all we could wish—such trees as one sees in dreams—and there we take the most picturesque breakfast in the world.

You are so comfortable with this extemporaneous Véfour, that you inevitably repeat the everlasting commonplace: "You feel at home there!" Indeed, the difficulty is, *not* to be comfortable!

Our presence in these unfrequented latitudes is a great puzzle to several little greenish cameleons, with red throats, who go out of their way expressly to see us eat, and seem to be saying to each other: "What the deuce have all these savages here come to do among us?"

The mute reflections of these young reptiles do not, however, prevent us from enjoying the mocha which our boatmen have taken the trouble to look up for us in a neighboring plantation.

After which, lighting an excellent regalia, we explore the heights in search of cocoa-nut trees; but the rascally cocoa-nuts are alike insensible to our blandishments and to the stones which we throw at them, and persist that they will not abandon the cocoa-nut tree which has given them birth.

It is an excellent trait of character. We understand it; and after crossing the village of Regia, a little place where negroes abound, we return to the city, where, just while we were felicitating ourselves on our country party, we perceive that the West India sun has tapped us on the head, and that we are slightly crazy.

You do not get sun strokes here, they are hammer strokes. So hard, that we are delirious all night, and get up a mass of dreams, every one of which is stupider than all the rest.

Next night, to complete our pleasure, the mulatresses by the side of us, the sheep, the horses, the cats and the watchmen, begin their thundering noise again, and will not be prevailed upon to stop until daybreak.

And this is not all. Hardly are these odious neighbors silent before a brigand of a cock takes it upon himself to sound the réveil! (Horrible animal! If that fellow keeps on crowing, what is the use of cock-fights?)

At this signal the parrot, (here we have something more which is amusing—parrots!) Bernard's parrot wakes up, and, without leaving his perch, begins with the parrotesses of the mulatresses (these dear little girls had parrots, too!) a conversation, in notes so piercing and so discordant, that all the poultry in the neighborhood felt it their duty to share in it!

And now, if you want to know why all this feathered population is indulging this morning in this musical dissipation, it is because to-day is the 30th of December, the festival of St. Columbus, and because St. Columbus's day is the birds' Christmas day! Every dog must have his day!

CHAPTER IX.

IN WHICH EVERYTHING RUNS ON FROM BAD TO WORSE.

On the first of January, 1856, Mademoiselle Rachel, remembering that it is New Year's day, sends to the artistes of her troupe, by way of New Year's presents, the following official news: That she, Mademoiselle Rachel, having formally declared that she would not play in Havana, the Félix enterprise existed no longer, and that, in consequence of this premature death, everybody, except herself, was to embark for New York on the 8th of that same month, and, on the 19th, take his final flight towards the flowery banks of the Seine!

On learning this irrevocable decree, the artists are horribly disappointed. From this moment salaries cease by the management.

Each one, therefore, has but one wish—to rescue himself as quickly as possible from this city, where nothing is doing, where nothing can be learned, and where everything begins to look black. I do not say this on account of the negroes here. Only on account of the yellow fever here, or vomito, just as you like, which one would be glad enough to die of, for a little while, considering the stifling heat of the winter which we enjoy this year.

And, by Hercules, this petty malady actually disturbs the composure of the company, who are not in very good health.

M. Félix, the father, among others, who is very much dissatisfied at having come so far as this with his numerous children, views this horrid yellow fever with an invincible antipathy, an insurmountable horror!

Ah! if he had only known, wouldn't he have staid in his country house at Montmorency with his hens!

He reproaches himself every day with having made this immense fiasco—he is not the only one.

Everybody is more or less vexed at being so thwarted, at having risked their necks fifty times, at risking them every day—and all that to arrive at a pecuniary result, which is nothing, compared with what everybody was to have had.

"Good God!" said some people, who knew nothing about our situation, to the artists, "you do not lose anything after all, by all this; you merely do not gain, that is all; while M. Raphaël Félix has lost all he had, and Mdlle. Rachel Félix will be compelled to loosen her purse-strings to send the company back to France."

The answer to this was, simply, that M. Raphaël Félix and his sister, having made an immense razzia of capital, in all their preceding excursions in France, in England, in Germany, in Italy, and, finally, in Russia, it was not a very bitter pill for them to leave a few hundred thousand francs with these *poor* Americans!

Pretty compassion, indeed, to bewail their lot! Why laugh at that? It is exactly as if, in a party at lansquenet, one should begin to lament the misfortune of a player, who lost a hundred sous after having gained a pile of a hundred louis.

Mdlle. Rachel and her brother have won

plenty of piles! They happen to lose one, the smallest of all; the public represents Charlemagne; every one plays as he understands it!

Meanwhile, we must say one thing; the Havana public would have been a good player and would have held out game till the party broke up.

The proof of which is, that they are actually furious at seeing the performances, which had been announced, fall to the ground so.

What, Rachel at Havana and they cannot hear Rachel! They think it altogether too much!

The French population (and that is tolerably numerous here) demand French pieces with all their might and main.

"If Rachel will not play," say they, "let the troupe play without her and everybody will come!"

I collar this idea, and make propositions to the manager of the Villanueva Theatre, which he accepts. After which I have the thing announced in the papers.

Unfortunately, it is not at all successful with the ex-members of the ex-French Company.

In general, these gentlemen prefer to regale themselves with a breath of French air; they think that Havana and the vomito together are decidedly too much of a good thing!

And then the real reason is, that Mdlle. Rachel formally opposes the artistes' playing without her at Havana! Why? Nobody knows! But she does oppose it, and as at present it is she who manages matters, pecuniarily speaking, instead of her brother Raphaël, some attention must be paid to her little whims. We shall, therefore, not play in any way on this unlucky island of Cuba.

Raphaël has been obliged to borrow of his sister. He *haaad* to come to it! *(il le fâaal-lait!)*

Or else he would have been very much embarrassed about paying M. Marty the forfeit, which he claims by law, 35,000 francs! That is for not having played! Well!

Then a very handsome collection of thousand franc bills must be disbursed for the company's voyage, and faith, thousand franc bills have had a final falling out with Raphaël.

So thoroughly that he sends his sister the

following note, which contains a detailed list of all the expenses which fall by necessity to her share! a list which she communicates to the artists next day, to prove to them that she, Rachel, and not he, Raphaël, pays this last money.

Here follows the note in question:

SUMS DUE AND SUMS NECESSARY.

	FRANCS.
Salaries of the Company, advances off (some for 25 days, others a month and a half) . .	25,082
Expenses at the hotels, from the day of the suspension of the salaries to the eighth of January, 1856, Hotel Legrand	1,950
Hotel Bernard (15 persons at 15 francs a day) .	3,875
Twenty-one passages from Havana to New York, at 300 francs -	6,300
Twenty-one passages to Liverpool, at 840 francs, .	16,600
Baggage	1,000
Baggage	2,500
Twenty persons from Liverpool to London, from London to Boulogne, and from Boulogne to Paris, 240 francs a head . . .	4,800
Baggage	1,000
Eight days at New York, waiting for the steamer, at 10 francs per day	2,000
Contingent expenses, of which an account will be rendered on arrival	2,000

All the above expenses are to be verified in Paris.

HAVANA, Jan. 2d, 1856.

DEBTS CONTRACTED IN NEW YORK.

D—— has lent to Mdlle. Rachel . . .	20,000
(*Note in Mdlle. Rachel's handwriting*, $4,000, which is more than 20,000 francs.)	
D—— has endorsed two letters of exchange .	11,000
Mdlle. Rachel owes M. Belmont, banker, . .	15,000
These three sums are borrowed, at 7 per cent. from the day of the loan.	
M. Marty, in Havana	35,000
Which makes the bagatelle of . .	148,107

At the end of this list, in a few lines written in her own hand, Mdlle. Rachel apprised us that none of these sums, of which her brother spoke, and which she had borrowed, had ever gone into his hands: "She must correct his management, but," she added, with an irony not very sisterly, "he is still all right, as it is I who pay!"

This list leaves us no longer the shadow of a doubt! We are going!

And we are to return to our *belle patrie* by way of New York.

New York! It is not more than half-pleasant to us to see this great Pandemonium again!

Our apprehensions do not last long! The

same day, the administration announces to us that we are not to go by way of the United States, but by the West India line! *Está bueno!*

Está bueno, is a Spanish word, which means *all right*. And "*all right*," it is high time to tell you, is an English word which represents, very stupidly, in the United States, the "*parfait! parfait! parfait! parfait!*" of Joseph Prudhomme.

CHAPTER X.

IN WHICH THE NEGROES ARE NOT SO VERY UNHAPPY AFTER ALL.

ALTHOUGH our route is changed, the sum of expenses remain about the same; the total is perhaps a little larger, that is all! However, I would not dare swear to that; but I am certain of this, it was impossible for us to get our passports on the day *de los Reyes*, under the specious pretext that it was the negro carnival! What a fine title for a drama, heigho!

THE NEGRO CARNIVAL!

This is a very curious festival, and it is peculiar to Havana.

From dawn of day all the slaves in the city are free, by law, until next morning.

If any master would compel one of them to work, the slave would go straightway to the Commissioner, and make his owner pay a thumping fine. These poor devils are all muffled up in the oddest costumes and the most impossible travesties, such as would be all the rage at a fancy ball.

I saw one with a genuine costume of a king of the middle ages, a very proper red, close coat, velvet vest, and a magnificent gilt paper crown. This negro, who was enormously tall, and had a tolerably good-looking head, gave his hand gravely to a sort of feminine blackamoor who represented some queen or other. He walked by her side with a deliberate, majestic step, never laughed, and seemed to be reflecting deeply on the grandeur of his mission to this world.

This temporary king was followed by a band of negroes, every one of whom was more hideous than all the rest, and was dressed in a more extravagant fashion.

Some had transformed themselves into South American savages, Red Skins, or Apaches. Others had been coquettishly affecting large yellow spots all over their body. In their hair they generally had magnificent peacock feathers, having destroyed all the dusters in the city. Most of them had flour on their faces. Myriads passed through the streets from morning till four o'clock, screeching out the songs of the country, with an accompaniment of rattles, tin pans and tambourines.

As they were passing before us, several of these crack-brains, in the hope of getting a few reals, undertook to give a diurnal serenade to Randoux, who was looking at them with a terribly haggard expression. It was, indeed, good and sufficient cause for going crazy, to listen to the unearthly sounds of their hoarse instruments, and their still hoarser voices.

Another negro, dressed in white and pale pink, with a shepherdess hat and a white and pink mask on his face, dropped on his knees before the Chéry brothers, and began to wipe their shoes with an embroidered handkerchief which he was flourishing pretentiously.

At four o'clock precisely they are prohibited from remaining in the city. They have no right to continue their procession, except outside of the barriers. There they riot all night, in the little holes which swarm in the lower streets beyond the barriers, and in the morning, at daybreak, they have to be at work again, or they had best beware the dance!

These fine negroes came into all the cafés,

all the shops; there they execute dances *à la* learned dog, and say to you, in airs that they improvise, compliments of this sort, which they have the audacity to print, and of which, if you have been generous with them, they leave you a copy in printing. Behold the poetry of these black skins:

"AGUINALDOS.

DECIMA.

"Yo que te doy á gustar
Mis manjares delicados,
Los que están bien cocinados
Porque los sé préparar;
Yo que agrado al paladar
Cuando desganado estás,
Hoy te vengo á implorar
Que el aguinaldo me des
Humilde, siempre á tus piés
Donde me puedes mandar.
Tu cocinero de apetito."

You don't know what these lines mean, do you? Well, I don't, either, and I don't care! I only put this ten-lined charabia before you to prove one thing, and that is, that the slaves in Havana have a good time, and that they are no so very unhappy, after all, since they devote themselves to belles lettres! Those who are really to be pitied, are the negroes on the sugar-plantations, in the interior of the island. While their brethren of the city are dancing to the sound of the tambourine, they have to work all the while, without rest or repose, to the less harmonious sound of the whip of their overseers.

"Miserable as a negro." This proverb is the product of a sugar plantation. So they abominate the whites—those fellows out there; the whites are their black beasts!

There is another thing, too, which they execrate, and that is the sugar-cane. They have a deep-rooted hatred for this American production. To such an extent that they will not sweeten the least drop of water with cane sugar. That would have upon them all the effect of poison. Their affection flows only in the direction of beet sugar!

It is this ugly culinary root alone which can destroy slavery on the western continent! This beet-root is a bloody abolitionist! And you will see, sooner or later, the black race will be raising statues to it!

CHAPTER XI.

IN WHICH WE ARE UP TO OUR NECKS IN FIGURES.

BEFORE bidding an everlasting adieu to this young and happy America, for we must bid adieu to this dear land, fate has resolved, with the concurrence of the great tragédienne, that we should indulge in a little figure-work—not very amusing to read, and certainly very tedious to write, but which seems to us to be an indispensable portion of this narrative.

We will give first, in one table, all the receipts of Rachel in New York and Boston, the only receipts of which we have the official figures, and we will place opposite, the receipts of Jenny Lind—so that one may comprehend at a glance, the very different results of these two gigantic enterprises:

RECEIPTS OF RACHEL, New York.			REC'TS OF JENNY LIND, New York.		
PERFORMANCES.	Dolls	Francs	Concerts.	Dolls	Francs
1 Horace	5,016	26,334	1	17,864	93,768
2 Phèdre	3,731	19,588	2	14,203	74,564
3 Adrienne	4,117	21,614	3	12,519	65,725

Rachel.	Dolls.	Francs.	Jenny Lind.	Dolls.	Francs.
4 Marie Stuart . . .	3,839	20,154	4	14,266	74,896
5 Adrienne	3,448	18,102	5	12,174	63,913
6 Horaces	3,675	19,293	6	16,028	84,147
7 Andromaque . . .	3,518	18,469	7	6,415	33,678
8 Angelo	3,518	18,469	8	4,009	25,725
9 Bajazet	3,505	18,401	9	5,982	31,405
10 Angelo	3,646	19,141	10	8,007	42,036
11 Phèdre	3,223	16,920	11	6,334	33,253
12 Adrienne	3,395	17,825	12	9,429	49,502
13 Andromaque . . .	2,326	12,211	13	9,912	52,038
14 Polyeucte . . .	2,625	13,781	14	5,775	30,307
15 Angelo	3,302	17,335	15	4,998	26,239
16 Marseillaise . . .	4,057	21,299	16	6,670	35,017
17 Marie Stuart . . .	2,857	14,999	17	9,840	51,660
18 Polyeucte	2,908	15,267	18	7,097	37,258
19 Jeanne d'Arc . . .	4,215	22,128	19	8,263	43,380
20 Adrienne	3,472	18,228	20	10,570	55,492
21 Phèdre	3,774	19,813	21	10,646	55,891
22 Adrienne	3,448	18,102	22	6,858	36,004
23 Horaces	3,097	16,259	23	5,453	28,627
24 Adrienne	1,624	8,526	24	5,463	28,679
25 Lady Tartuffe . . .	1,622	8,515	25	6,858	36,004
26 Angelo	2,668	14,007	26	5,453	28,627
27 Virginie	2,465	12,941	27	5,463	28,679
28 Mdlle. de Belle-Isle	3,002	15,760	28	7,378	38,734
29 Phèdre	3,924	20,601	29	7,179	37,689
30 Reading	1,578	8,284	30	6,641	34,865
31 Reading			31	7,179	37,689
Total	97,595	512,363		264,924	1,395,509

Boston.			Boston.		
1 Horaces	3,782	19,855	1	16,479	86,514
2 Phèdre	3,726	19,561	2	11,848	62,202
3 Angelo	3,397	17,834	3	8,639	45,354
4 Andromaque . . .	3,916	20,559	4	10,169	53,387
5 Marie Stuart . . .	3,428	17,997	5	10,524	55,251
6 Adrienne	3,214	16,873	6	5,240	27,510
7 Polyeucte, le Moineau de Lesbie . . .	800	4,200	7	7,586	39,826
Total . . .	22,263	116,879		70,485	370,044

Recapitulation.

	Dolls.	Francs.	Dolls.	Francs.
New York	97,595	512,363	264,924	1,395,509
Boston	22,263	116,879	70,485	370,044
Total	119,758	629,242	335,409	1,765,553

The Swedish Nightingale having given but

seven concerts in Boston, our comparative view breaks off at the seventh night of Mdlle. Rachel; we have, therefore, to add to this total of

	629,242 francs,
The receipts of the eighth night in Boston, (*Adrienne*)	15,960
As well as the receipts of the ninth night, (*Virginie*)	18,831
Plus the receipts in Philadelphia, proximate, and not official, (*Horaces*) . . .	10,000
And, finally, the receipts still more proximate, and still less official, in Charleston, (*Adrienne*)	10,000
Which gives for the Félix enterprise, the definite result of	684,033 francs

Which is not to be sneezed at—very hard.

I do not speak here of what was made by the sale of those horrid English translations which imitated rain so splendidly, and the beauties of Racine and Corneille so pitifully.

In the first place, this was a separate piece of business, and then, I believe that all that could have been made was not more than enough to pay the expenses of the Spanish translations, not one of which brought a sou, as may well be supposed, and which were sold by weight for waste paper to an apothecary in

Havana. How flattering to our great French poets!

Ah! we had a grudge against them for not being able to make themselves appreciated in the United States! We had our revenge! O ingratitude of mortals.

However, say what you will against these poor tragedies, still by their aid, and that of Adrienne Lecouvreur, Mdlle. Rachel must have pocketed in America, according to the terms of her engagement, an amount with which, considering the shortness of the time, a young man out of place ought to be tolerably well contented.

You can easily convince yourself of this by casting your eyes over a few figures, a little lower down, which we have ennuyéed ourselves in arranging.

"Ah! too many figures!" do you say. That is precisely our opinion; but we are ahead of you. It is our business here to be chin-deep in arithmetic, and we shall be so through this whole chapter; here is the proof of it:

Twenty-nine nights in New York, at 6,000 francs a night, ... 174,000 francs.

A benefit in addition, guaranteed to pay 20,000 francs, ...	20,000
(You will remember that Mdlle. Rachel gave up her claim for the second reading; that is why we count only thirty nights here.)	
Eight nights in Boston, ...	54,000
A benefit in addition, ...	20,000
One night in Philadelphia, . . .	6,000
One night in Charleston, . . .	6,000
Total,	280,000 francs.

I repeat it, a man terribly hard up would be satisfied with these few sous.

Over and above that, I believe that the administration paid Mdlle. Rachel two or three sums of 6,000 francs apiece (never anything but 6,000 francs; it is a stereotyped sum, like the price of small pies), for performances which were advertised but not given, from some cause not proceeding from Mdlle. Rachel. Which would raise the grand total to 298,000 francs (figures forever!). After all, this total is very fair for playing only forty-two nights!

Yes; but look at the reverse of the medal. This poor product must be abridged nearly half to pay a little bill of expense, which you will find a little way back, if you take the trouble to look a moment, amounting to 148,107 francs, and which reduces the savings of Mdlle. Rachel to 149,893 francs.

And we have here taken into consideration:

Neither the 5,000 francs sent to the sufferers in Norfolk.

Nor the 800 francs given to the sailors' orphans.

Nor the indispensable presents and compulsory generosities; nor the cost of costumes (which must amount to considerable, as Mdlle. Rachel had an entire new wardrobe, made in honor of the Americans).

Nor, the innumerable visits of her innumerable physicians! which costs roundly in America, I beg you to believe.

It would be horridly dear to die there, according to the rules of the profession! You would find it almost as cheap to live.

Which proves by A plus B, that Mdlle. Rachel is very far from carrying away from the New World the 1,200,000 fixed upon in her engagement, and the 80,000 francs which this generous engagement guaranteed her, in addition, for her four benefit nights!

And now, thank God, we have done with figures! Ouf!

CHAPTER XII.

IN WHICH MDLLE. RACHEL THINKS HER COMPANY MIGHT AS WELL MOVE ON.

MDLLE. RACHEL, who at first thought she would remain alone in the Island of Cuba, and let us come home to France without her, announces to us the night before this memorable retreat, that she will actually embark with us.

She is right. The weather is beginning to be rather bad, the Gulf of Mexico is already amusing itself by grumbling, and, before long, this blackguard Atlantic will be getting his back up.

At Havana there are, now and then, frightful storms, in comparison with which all the old deluges are nothing at all.

There is a foot of water in the streets; the whole city is navigable. These floods, too, have their good side. They wash this good capital, to which, in spite of all my affection for it, I cannot help giving hereby a certificate of filthiness, with the guarantee of the government. It would be so easy to sweep it a little! But they have so much else to do.

First of all, they must sleep. Everything else can be put off till another time! The more I reflect on the subject, the more I am convinced that the genuine citizen of Havana resembles that intelligent gnawer of the dormouse family, called by naturalists, a marmot, and by Savoyards, their friend.

There is only this slight difference between the two—the marmot sleeps in winter alone, the denizen of Havana sleeps summer and winter. And they are chilly in this country. The storm brought a little cooler weather, very little cooler. Well, all these white clothes suddenly disappear. People are muffled up. They cover their noses. Rabbit-skin gloves make their appearance, and chafing dishes are to be seen everywhere.

The negroes, especially, look as if they were freezing. The poor creatures have wrapped themselves up in immense Spanish cloaks, which gives them the most ludicrous awkwardness imaginable. One would think it was freezing as hard as possible, and yet we are enjoying delightfully mild weather, like that of Paris in July, not later!

Before finally setting out for this last-named capital, the land of promise to so many of us, we were very far from thinking that we should yet have another account to settle with tragedy; but we were mistaken.

In a creole family where we lived, Randoux (appropriately surnamed "the terror of serpents) and I were compelled to enact by turns scenes of the Horatii and Curiatii, Nemours and Polyeucte, which produced great effect, and convinced me still more that we should have realized here enormous sums, if we had played.

I will say, furthermore, that tragedy, which puts the northern Americans so soundly asleep, acts altogether differently on the charming *Havanese*, who listened to us without understanding, expressing their approbation so comically at the end of each verse which appeared good to them. Corneille would scarcely have expected such success as this! That comes of travelling!

Be consoled Corneille! to-day is the 10th of January, and thy Rachel, as weary as thyself of this unprofitable exile, will take thee back to thy well-beloved France! She has said so! she will embark with us!

The vessel in which we set out is none other than the steamer of the Antilles. It has come from Vera Cruz, and will touch at the island of St. Thomas. This boat is called the *Clyde.*

Is it because this name is the same as that of a river in Scotland, or for some other reason? At all events, at the moment of departure, Mademoiselle Rachel sends us a second announcement, as she did yesterday, and yet not like that of yesterday.

Waves and women are ever varying, and, this time, she has *re*-decided, that, until further notice, she will remain in Havana.

Fiat voluntas sua!

Poor Corneille!

And that is why the unfortunate French Company, which embarked so smart, so delighted, so self-confident, for the nation of millions, left, once for all, the port of Havana, half gay, half sad, altogether undeceived in respect of the gold mines of the other world, and, above all, without its *grande tragédienne!*

Ninth Part.

FROM THERE, HERE.

CHAPTER I.

IN WHICH WE SPEAK OF THE "PACIFIC," AND, NATURALLY, OF SHIPWRECKS.

MADEMOISELLE RACHEL has a fixed determination to return to Europe in the *Pacific*, the famous steamer which brought us to America.

Poor *Pacific!* Everybody knows that she is lost, crew and cargo.

She left Liverpool on the 23rd of January; on the 15th of April nothing had been heard of her. Eighty-two days instead of eleven. There is now not the least ray of hope.

What a terrible thing the ocean is!

Mademoiselle Rachel is not the only one who did not take her departure on board the *Clyde*.

Her sister Sarah embarked that same morning on the *Isabel*, also our comrade Randoux.

Mademoiselle Sarah will stop in Charleston; Randoux will go back to New York on business. Painful necessity!

Mesdemoiselles are also en route for that *triste* city of New York on board the *Granada*, a horrible boat, a real pasteboard steamer, a stage property, which, after several days' voyage, will play out its last farce by wrecking itself and throwing its passengers overboard.

A charming jest, especially in winter, which the United States steamers indulge in very often. Those which do not run you aground, blow you up. Take your choice! Oh! American boats! There is something to beware of!

I read lately that in 1849, of 1656 steamboats on the Mississippi, (the Mississippi only, you understand,) 736 had been destroyed—681 by explosion and 45 by collision. In 1851 the total of the list of lost boats was 1,390.

Since 1853, the United States have lost twelve large steamers, valued at 7,250,000 dollars, and 1,250 people perished in these shipwrecks.

In 1853, the *Independence*, having 120 passengers on board; the *Tennessee* and the *St. Louis* were lost, crews and cargoes, in the Pacific. The *Humboldt* and the *San Francisco* were wrecked in 1854 in the Atlantic; in the following year, the *Franklin*, the *City of Philadelphia* and the *Yankee Blade* were also lost, and the loss of the *City of Glasgow*, and that of the *Arctic* completed the melancholy list of disasters in 1854. The year 1855, with the wreck of the *North Carolina* and that of the *Golden Age*, which, however, has been raised and repaired. Finally, the year 1856 begins with the loss of this same *Pacific* of which we spoke at first. Sad début!

Well, at least with the English you are safe! for one reason, that there is on board all these steamers the same discipline as on men-of-war, and, I tell you, without such discipline there is everything to be feared. When the Arctic was wrecked, if she had been manned with true sailors, all her passengers would have been saved! On board the Clyde, we have a quantity of guns, of pistols, hatchets, and sabres. This arsenal is to be used not only to defend herself against pirates who rove from time to time in the sea of the Antilles, but in case of a mutiny among the crew, the passengers have orders to arm themselves and to lend a strong hand to the command. *All right!* (There is some English again!)

CHAPTER II.

IN WHICH WE PASS BY MONSIEUR SOULOUQUE.

The *Clyde* would be a perfect boat if one could only sleep a little on board of her! Sleep!—For six months we haven't known what that is! It is one of the greatest miseries of these voyages.

So, on the *Clyde*, it was insupportable. All night long the bawling of two babies mingled with the monotonous and incessant cough of two Americans afflicted with old age and catarrh.

Add to that the continual howling of a horrid little dog which M. Félix (son) had brought from Havana in a basket, and you will have a faint idea of the deplorable charivari which drove us mad every night.

Thank God, the *Clyde* made good speed, and on the 13th we doubled the point of the island of Cuba, in one of those Senegambian heats which the sea of the Antilles knows so well how to produce.

The sea of the Antilles! Here is a sea, a real sea, will you hear about that?

On the morning of the 14th, we ran along the coasts of St. Domingo, or Hayti, if you like it better, the empire of Papa Soulouque, a huge black, who runs in debt everywhere, and who sells his subjects to keep himself out of Clichy.

As we were passing by the states of the above-named gentleman, we were induced to read again the following letter, which may give an idea of the manner in which the good little Faustin treats good little whites:

"Last May the Haytiens arrested eight or ten Frenchmen, *born in the Antilles*, to enlist them in the Haytien army. These young men, on their refusal to adopt the military dress, were dragged to prison, and put into a dungeon in rons, where they remained five days.

"Thanks to the intervention of the vice-consul, M. E. Wielt, sole agent at that time, the prisoners were set at liberty, but were forbidden to continue their business. Those who were clerks were discharged by their employers, those who were merchants were compelled to close their shops.

"In July several officers of a man-of-war, the *Chimère*, were walking through the streets of Port-au-Prince. Being summoned by some sentinels to throw away their cigars, they thought they were near a powder-magazine, and obeyed orders.

"'Hats off, do you not hear, hats off before the emperor's house!' they then cried out; and on their refusal to salute the dwelling of the chief, who had gone to the little Goâve, were about to take them to prison. One of these young seamen, knowing that he was quite in the power of these brutes, demanded to be carried before the governor. And he had the good sense to send them to the consulate.

"Monsieur de Chacon, secretary to the Spanish consulate, came from the Minister of Foreign Affairs, where he had been to solicit of the Emperor Faustin an audience for his consul. Going out, he did what everybody would do under a sun at thirty-seven degrees—he put on his hat. Immediately the sentinels vociferate their insolent order, 'hats off!' M. de Chacon refuses to salute the walls. The same scene, the same noise and scandal for him as for the officers of the *Chimère*. But this time the emperor appeared at the window; and when he hears what it is about, he cried out, *Mille tonnerres*, don't you know me? salute my house, or I will throw you into prison.' The advisers of his Imperial Majesty observed to him, that this arrest could not be executed on the person of a chancellor without leading to the most serious consequences. It was, nevertheless, only after twenty minutes' parleying that the soldiers liberated M. de Chacon!" How amiable the fat black is!

We entertain, for an instant, the idea of giving ourselves a closer view of this kingdom of Chinese shadows; but, as that would take us a precious time, we pass on, and the next day we are in sight of Porto-Rico, one of the Great Antilles, where the cholera rages with horrible violence, having already destroyed two-thirds of the population!

Let us go on quickly!

CHAPTER III.

EN ROUTE FOR EUROPE.

In the night, we arrive before the island of St. Thomas, where we land in the morning, at sunrise.

At St. Thomas, it is a different thing: not the least cholera, but yellow fever to a frightful degree.

We embark instantly on the *Atrato*, an immense English steamer, commanded by an excellent captain, whose name I regret exceedingly not to be able to give you.

There they stop the dog of M. Félix. They demand 100, or 125 francs, I believe, for his passage.

M. Félix, seeing that he can no longer keep his odious quadruped, except by making a sacrifice, does not hesitate a second, and presents his animal to a gentleman who remains in St. Thomas. This desertion causes us only very moderate grief. We are, for the most part, satisfied to be rid of this nocturnal bore. It is, at least, one less.

This happy incident sends us to the table with unusual cheerfulness!

What a difference there is between English and American boats, in respect of the fare!

On American boats, as we have said, the meats are killed in advance, preserved in ice, and, consequently, horrid, both in taste and aspect. On the English, the meats are put on board alive, and it is very comforting, very enlivening, I assure you, to see on deck these regiments of sheep, hens, turkeys, ducks, and even turtles. It is actually a menagerie, which lessens every day, at a frightful rate.

As everybody is sick upon this voyage, we suppose we shall not escape more than the others.

But we are now old sailors, and enjoy audacious health, which prevents us from ever missing a meal.

This extraordinary appetite does not fail to seriously alarm the cook on board.

In case of shipwreck, what would become

of us, *bon Dieu?* Happily for everybody, the gallant *Atrato* enters the port of Southampton on the appointed day—that is, on the 31st of January, 1856!

Europe! Here we are! It is not a dream! Such is life, however—and steam!

Just to think, only six months and three days, to a day, since we climbed into the cars of the railroad *du Nord*—indulging aside in the consoling reflection, that we shall, perhaps, never again drive over the Macadam of our boulevards.

And this reflection was a perfectly true one —we are convinced of it now. For the countries in which we have just travelled are dangerous. And the Americans themselves agree to that.

One of them, a Yankee, who spoke French, almost, when I asked what I had better take to France, as curiosities from the New World, "My dear sir," he replied, rolling a large "quid" of tobacco in his mouth, "there is only one truly curious thing that Europeans can carry home with them when they have travelled in America, that is—their skin!"

For this reason the French Company were delighted even to reach England—two steps, so to speak, from France, from Paris, the only country which is unexceptionably beautiful and good, and which one never loves more than when away from it.

Raphaël Félix alone wears a sad countenance, which contrasts singularly with the joyous faces of all the rest. The tables are turned.

He has something to be terribly mortified about, besides! It was so easy to have remained all comfortably in France, and not to have put his nose in America!

But you wanted to, Raphaël!

And superstitious people, who are as stubborn as red asses, say that all would have run as smoothly as little wheels, if we had not left France on a FRIDAY.

CHAPTER IV.

MADEMOISELLE RACHEL WRITES IN THE PAPERS.

To reassure her friends of the health of Mademoiselle Rachel, we append a note from our friend Bernard:

"HAVANA, *January* 28, 1856.

"Our celebrated tragédienne embarks this very day for New York. The day after our departure, she left the Marty's house, to go to Mr. O'Farril's. She longed to recite something for them, so she gave *le Songe d'Athalie* (for O'Farril's family only). She wished to have a reception, but could not. She intended to remain much longer in this family, but home-sickness seized her, and—"

And here she is, back again in France, in her little house at Meulan—very much disgusted with having made such a voyage, and

"Jurant, mais un peu tard, qu'on ne l'y prendra plus."

To cap the climax, some one amuses himself by writing in the newspapers that she is about to yield herself up to the sweet bonds of Hymen. Whereupon she is greatly provoked, and replies at once—a charming letter, which it is a pleasure to us, as well as a duty, to reproduce here:

"I have heard many clever people say that it was often better to be abused by the press, than to incur its silence and neglect. But why, my dear friend, should you have busied yourself so long in inventing marriage plans to twit me with, and why attribute to me a thing so useless?

"I have two sons whom I adore. I am thirty-two years old by my register of birth; I look fifty, and as for the rest I will not say much. Eighteen years of tearing passions to tatters on the stage, of mad scamperings to the ends of the earth, of Moscow winters, of Waterloo betrayals, the perfidious sea, the ungrateful land,—these are the things which wrinkle before her time a poor little bit of a woman like me. But God shields the brave, and he seems to have created, expressly for me, a little corner unknown to all the geographies, where I can forget my fatigues, my troubles, my premature old age. And yet you let fly your rascally canard in the midst of the birds which perch on my branches, and sing nice little songs of a return — not mine, probably, but spring's.

"If I had died in America, you would have been the first —oh, I am quite sure of it!—to dedicate to me one of your most glowing feuilletons—worthy of your talents, and just like your heart. And now, because I am raised from the dead after a miraculous fashion, because I can hope to see you once more, and shake hands with my old friend, you say to yourself 'she's alive and well, thank God! now, to tease her!' Then you go to work again to irritate my too susceptible nerves, and amuse people at the expense of poor little Rachel. A pretty triumph for your genius—as if there were any lack of victims! Is that the way you should behave to a poor thing who has actually come back from *the other world?* Come, be good now, and quickly confess yourself guilty of inveterately teasing poor little me, so that I, also, may promptly forgive you—once more, and hope soon to see you again in Paris or the country.

"By Jupiter, I think it is very nice of me to treat you thus, for this letter is certainly not written by a *Grand Tragédienne,* but by a good child who is called

"RACHEL."

While the pen was in her hand, what a charming occasion to write to her ex-pensioners that she held at their disposal some paltry thousand franc bills, which they expected for the London performances.

CHAPTER V.

HOW ALL FINISHES WITH A LAWSUIT.

As well as his illustrious daughter, M Félix is deeply vexed at having made this useless excursion, and when some one met him on the Boulevard, and began to ask him for the news:

"Don't speak to me of the expedition to America," cried he, "or I will have you arrested."

And, the other day, about to start for his country seat: "I really do not dare to return to Montmorency," said he, retracing his steps; "I shall be badgered by my very hens!"

As to Mademoiselle Rachel's sister, Mademoiselle Sarah, she is now in New York, as well as Mademoiselles Durrey and Briard, the two wrecked ones of the *Granada*.

We learn that Mademoiselle Sarah, who is not engaged in the United States, as we had written, will be in Paris before long, to form a dramatic troupe, with the intention of taking it to America. Good luck to her!

Because Mademoiselle Rachel did not return to France with all of us, there have been a thousand ridiculous rumors afloat here.

They even went so far as to say that the great tragédienne would not put her foot in Paris, for fear of a lawsuit against her, which several of her company intended to prosecute.

That rumor was entirely false then. But to-day it is no longer so. It is not the artists who prosecute the lawsuit (the American business, moreover, was previously settled, as to them, and there was nothing more to pay for, except that eternal month in London, of which we spoke in the last of the preceding chapter). But here comes, from America, M. Gustave Naquet, ex-minister plenipotentiary of Raphaël Félix, who is favored with a blazing disgrace scarcely two months after our arrival in the United States, and who is anxious to show up this disgrace to the Parisian tribunals.

As soon as he arrives in Paris, he sends to

Gustave Bourdin, one of the Editors-in-chief of the *Figaro*, the following letter—

A M. Gustave Bourdin.

"MY DEAR FRIEND—Since you are one of the very holy and very *spirituelle* trinity which presides over the destinies of the *Figaro*, permit me to take advantage of our old fellowship in journalism to place before the public a report against the Félix family in general, and M. Raphaël Félix in particular.

"You know that, yielding to the temptation of certain notes of prospective thousands, I mixed myself up with this tragic exploring expedition, the catastrophes of which Léon Beauvallet has narrated with as much wit as good-humor. At first, I was to have no other duties except those of interpreter, on account of my acquaintance with the English language; and it was perfectly understood, between M. Raphaël and myself, that my name should not appear in any connection. So well understood, that, in the list of *personnel* published by the *Figaro* before the departure of the troupe for America, I am designated only by my Christian name.

"But I could not long preserve my incognito in my unforeseen departments of general agent, private attorney—what not?—the Jack-of-all-trades to M. Raphaël Félix. I took my duties upon myself immediately, and I did my best to prepare for Mademoiselle Rachel a profitable campaign in the New World. They made me so many fine promises! My plans had succeeded perfectly. The biography of Mirecourt was crushed under an artistic one of Mademoiselle Rachel written by me in English. The press of New York, which gives the key-note to the whole press of the United States, had sung thousands and thousands of times the praises of Rachel; and, on the coming of the great tragédienne, the public was disposed to applaud her, and to pay very dear for the right of going to the theatre.

"The success was, I must say, immense—an artistic and lucrative success—and that, in spite of the administrative peculiarities of M. Raphaël Félix, who possessed a remarkable talent for making enemies of the press and the public. His blunders were without numher, and some of his financial transactions produced a scorching letter from the Honorable Fernando Wood, mayor of the city of New York, in which that functionary, more severe than the mayor of Meaux, sharply rebuked the European Bilboquet, and recalled him to the modesty of his position.

"I have not time to-day to enter into details, which would not be wanting in interest, in respect of art and to artists who think of visiting the new world. I will only say that after ten or eleven weeks Mademoiselle Rachel was able to send to Europe a draft for three hundred thousand francs, and M. Raphaël one of sixty thousand.

"Since then, as Mademoiselle Rachel has been ill, she must have disbursed about one hundred and fifty thousand francs, and I have not heard that M. Raphaël has disbursed anything at all. How, then, does it happen, that this gentleman goes about, telling everybody that he has lost three hundred thousand francs, and his sister as much more? Is it by way of replying in advance to the demands of his artists, on the subject of sums due for the month in London, or some other reason? I don't know. At all events, there can be nothing falser.

"I come now to what concerns me in all this: finding myself compelled to reply, once for all, to the reports circulated about me by M. Raphael Felix, since his return, and which have been attested by twenty reliable witnesses. M. Raphaël has conducted himself towards me in a manner which I could not properly describe, without going beyond the bounds you have assigned me.

"He left me, for some trifling pretext, in Philadelphia, on the 15th of November, and since that time, he has sent me no money at all, not even that which was necessary to take me back to Paris. He laughs at the contract he has made with me, knowing very well it was impossible for me to require the adherence to it, by law in America, where, as a foreigner, I should be compelled, before proceeding, to furnish bail to the amount of fifty thousand francs.

" He has slandered me in Paris to our mutual friends, to justify his conduct, and he thinks I will recoil from the scandal, the costs, and the tediousness, of a lawsuit, to obtain justice. He is mistaken, and by no manner of means shall I shrink from anything to obtain satisfaction for the procedures which he has employed against me. Moreover, to gain at once my cause before the public, before the Courts have decided, I here make a proposition to M. Raphaël Félix, which I dare him to accept.

" I propose to him to designate, himself, two arbitrators among men of letters or artists, the most honorably known in Paris, and let us leave to their decision our common grievances.

" I accept in advance those he may choose as judges, satisfied that he cannot find two men of intelligence and honor, who, on examining the documents, will not declare that M. Raphaël Felix has conducted himself shamefully towards me, and that he owes me the indemnification specified in our treaty.

" By giving space in the next number to this letter, written in such haste at the moment of arriving from the New World, you will oblige your old comrade,

" Gustave Naquet."

I must mention that I wrote at once to this same Naquet, to find out what had occasioned this rather warm epistle. Here is his reply : it is of the same temperature.

"My Dear Beauvallet:

"You ask me what has become of my affair with the Félix family. Of course, M. Raphaël did not reply to the loyal proposition I made him. It enters, perhaps, into the calculations of this *Monsieur*, who calls himself ruined, to pass for being too poor to buy somebody's style and orthography—those two accomplishments not yet making a part of the brilliant education of M. Raphaël. The law will then take its course, and the public will soon be made acquainted with this *Martial* family of the dramatic art, in which, *L'Ile des Ravageurs* is called tragedy. This will form the natural finis of your little book, in which you do not seem to me to have done justice to the American public, which, called upon to pay and applaud the Rachel of former days, did come, notwithstanding the worthless representations of her man-of-straw, her speculator-director.

"I press your hand.

"Gustave Naquet."

CHAPTER VI.

WHICH SUDDENLY FINDS ITSELF THE LAST OF ALL.

As the reader has easily perceived by what he has just read, Naquet is decidedly not in a good-humor with Mdlle. Rachel and her family. In compliance with his request, we have, nevertheless, thought it a duty to publish this letter. We can so much the less decline to do so, that he accuses us, in his reply, of having, to a degree, deceived our readers as to Mdlle. Rachel's reception by the Americans. We have but one answer to that: the figures are there—a very pretty table—you have only to contemplate them. Certainly, we entertain for the North Americans only a very limited admiration; but, throughout this volume, it may be seen, that we would catch on the wing the least occasion to speak well of them.

We have rendered to the Press of the New World full and complete justice—everybody knows that; and it is only the masses that we have attacked. As for all those details of murders, arsons, etc., etc., we have merely related the facts, not a word more. *Pardieu*, you have only to read the American newspapers, and you will see; only, over there, it is spoken of as quite natural, while here we take the pains to underscore it; that is all. As for the rest, we have in our possession the very journals of which we have spoken, and, if need be, they shall bear us witness.

Now, to wind up in the true American fashion, I am going to treat you to one of the prettiest canards that has been hatched this long time. Méry is father to it, as *Figaro* informs us.

"The public has for some time been the victim of a double mystification. Madame Ristori has no more gone to Italy than Mademoiselle Rachel to America. They have both passed the last nine months in delightful companionship in a charming villa at Pantin, where they have whiled away the time in reciprocally instructing each other in their respective languages. Only, their success has not been commensurate with their efforts, and has produced a curious result. Mademoiselle Rachel has forgotten French, and Madame Ristori no longer knows a word of Italian!"

While I am borrowing for the last time from *Figaro*, let me profit by the occasion to thank him for the hospitality he has hitherto extended to me, and to congratulate him upon all the good luck which has fallen to his lot. He deserves it.

15 April (*jour du terme!*).

THE END.

www.ingramcontent.com/pod-product-compliance
Lightning Source LLC
LaVergne TN
LVHW020057110826
845151LV00001B/7

* 9 7 8 1 4 2 5 5 4 5 1 7 8 *